baby names

baby names

more than 3000 names, with origins and meanings

Laura Emerson

LONDON • NEW YORK

Dedication

To my wonderful husband,
for your support in all things.

Senior designer Toni Kay
Picture research Christina Borsi
Production Gary Hayes
Art director Leslie Harrington
Editorial director Julia Charles

First published in 2013 by
Ryland Peters & Small
20–21 Jockey's Fields
London WC1R 4BW
and
519 Broadway, Fifth Floor
New York, NY 10012
www.rylandpeters.com

Text copyright ©
Laura Emerson 2013

Design and illustrations
copyright © Ryland Peters
& Small 2013

10 9 8 7 6 5 4 3 2

ISBN 978-1-84975-372-2

Printed and bound in China.

A CIP record for this book is
available from the British Library.

Contents

Introduction

How do you give someone you've only just met a name that fits and will last them a lifetime? This is the daunting yet exciting task that faces all new parents. In the past, parents tended to use a family name or picked one from a handful of choices that expressed their religious beliefs. Today, the same may still be true for many of us, but more often new parents are searching among a sea of choices to find the 'perfect' name that possesses all the right qualities and positive associations. That's not a bad thing, but as a result it seems as if perhaps there's more pressure today than there used to be.

Choosing a name for your baby doesn't have to be as challenging as it first seems. In fact, everyone has a naming style, even if it doesn't seem obvious at first. You will discover that you naturally gravitate toward names with a certain sound, origin, or meaning. Browsing through different options will often lead to the perfect name for baby emerging as you go about your day. In the end, the right name will be the one that you love the best. Bear in mind that it has to sound right with your last name, and remember to avoid initials that create embarrassing words or acronyms.

In this book, you'll find just the right number of names to choose from. Whether you're looking for something classic, old-fashioned, international, trendy, biblical, nature-related, or unique, you'll find it here. Along with the names you'll also find a few themed lists to get your creative juices flowing.

Naming your child should be a pleasureable process with a wonderful result – a name that you will both love and enjoy for the rest of your lives. With the help of this book, I hope that's exactly what happens for you.

Elizabeth

Angelique   Lilly   Rosie

Girls Names

Willow   Zoe   Gwynneth

Barbara   Brylee   Lydia

Agnes   Madeline

Charlee   Deanna

Eve

Jemma

Lauren

Josephine   Charlotte   Nyla

A

Aaliyah (Hebrew)
To ascend.

Aberdeen (Scottish)
A city in Scotland,
named for the meeting
of two rivers.

Abia (Arabic) Great.

Abigail (Hebrew)
A Biblical name meaning
father's joy. *Abby,
Abigale, Avigail*

Abrielle (Hebrew)
Mother of multitudes.
From Abra, the feminine
form of Abraham. *Abra,
Abréa, Abreana, Abria*

Acacia (Greek) Name
of the acacia tree.

Ada (German) Nobility.

Adalyn (Hebrew) God is
my refuge. A variation of
Adalia, but also inspired
by the name Madeline.
Adalia, Adalie

Addison (English) Son
of the mighty warrior.
Inspired by the surname
Madison.

Adelaide (German)
Noble, kind. Newly stylish
again since its high point
in the 1800s.

Adele, **Adella** (German)
Nobility.

Adeline (French) Nobility.
Diminutive of Adele.
Adelina, Adelyn

Adelpha (Greek) Caring sister. *Delfa, Delpha*

Adora (Latin) Adored. *Adore, Adoria, Dora*

Adriana, Adrienne (Latin) Black earth. The feminine form of Adrian. *Adria, Adriena*

Africa The continent.

Afton (Scottish) A river in Scotland, made famous by the poet Robert Burns.

Agape, Agapi (Greek) Love.

Agatha (Greek) Good. *Agace, Agasha, Aggie*

Agave (Greek) Noble. Also the name of a plant and nectar.

Agnes (Greek) Virginal, chaste. *Agnesa, Agnola, Nesa, Senga, Ynes*

Agrippa (Latin) Born feet-first. *Agrafina, Agrippina*

Ailani (Hawaiian) Chief. *Aelani, Ailana*

Ailbhe (AL-va) (Irish) Noble, bright. *Alva*

Aileen (Irish) Light. Variation of Helen.

Ailey (French) Light. Variation of Aileen.

Ailsa (Scottish) Place name referring to Ailsa Craig, an island in Scotland.

Aimée (French) Beloved. French version of Amy.

Ainsley (Scottish) A meadow. *Ainslee, Ainslie, Ansley*

Aiofe (EE-fa) (Irish) Radiant, beautiful.

Airlea (Greek) Ethereal.

Aisha (Arabic) Woman. The name of Muhammad's favourite wife.

Aisling (ASH-ling) (Irish) Dream, vision.

Aislinn (ASH-lyn) (Irish) Dream. Variation of Aisling. *Ashlyn, Ashlynn*

Aithne (ETH-na) (Irish) Fire. Feminine version of Aidan.

Aiyana (Native American) Eternal blossom.

Akira (Japanese) Intelligent, bright.

Alabama (Native American) Debated meaning. A place name with southern pride.

Alaina, Alayna (French) Bright, shining.

Alana (Irish) Fair. Feminine form of Alan. *Alannah, Alanna*

Alani (Hawaiian) Orange tree.

Alanis (Irish) Variation of Alana.

Alaya (Hebrew) To ascend. *Alayah*

Alba (English) Town on a white hill. Featured in the novel *The Time Traveler's Wife*.

Albany (English) Place name from the state of New York.

Alberta (English) Noble. Feminine form of the less elegant Albert.

Alea (Arabic) Honourable. *Aleah, Aleigha, Alia, Aliya, Aliyah*

Alena (Greek) Light. Variation of Helen.

Alegria (Spanish) Joy. *Alegra, Allegria*

Alexandra (Greek) Man's defender. *Alexis, Alexia, Alexa, Alessandra, Alex, Alejandra*

Aliana (Greek) Light. Often cited as a variation of Helen or Alana.

Alice (German) Noble. This name became a classic after achieving popularity in the 1950s.

Alicia (English) Noble. A variation of Alice.

Alina (Russian) Nobility, light.

Alisha (Sanskrit) Protected by God. Also a spelling variation of Alicia.

Alison (French) Noble. Variation of Alice. *Allison, Alyson, Ali, Allie*

Alissa (English) Noble. Variation of Alice. *Alyssa*

Alita (Spanish) Nobility.

Alivia (Latin) Olive tree. Up-and-coming variation inspired by Olivia. *Alyvia*

Aliza (Hebrew) Joyful.

Alizée (al-ee-ZAY) (French) Trade wind.

Allegra (Italian) Joyful.

Allete (French) Winged one.

Alma (Latin) Nurturing one.

Aloisia (German) Famous fighter.

Alondra (Greek) Man's defender. A Spanish variation of Alexandra.

Alora (American) A created name stemming from Lora, a variation of Laura.

Alona (Hebrew) Oak tree. *Allona, Alonia*

Amalia (Latin) Industrious. Variation of Emily.

Amanda (Latin) Loved. *Amandi, Amandine, Amata, Manda, Mandy*

Amani (Arabic) Faith.

Amara (Greek) Lovely, immortal.

Amari (Hebrew) Eternal.

Amaya (Japanese) Night rain.

Amber (English) Semi-precious stone. *Amberly*

Ambrosia (Greek) Food of the gods.

Amelia, Amelie (Latin) Industrious. A variation of Emily.

America (English) Ruler of the home. A name that peaked after 9/11.

Amethyst (English) Semi-precious stone.

Amina (Arabic) Honest.

Amira (Arabic) Leader. *Amirah*

Amissa (Hebrew) Friend.

Amity (Latin) Friendship. A pretty and unexpected virtue name.

Amiya (Indian) Delight. Amiyah

Amor, Amora (Spanish) Love.

Amy (Latin) Beloved. Short and sweet. *Amie, Aimée, Amelia, Amata*

Ana, Anna (Hebrew) Grace. A variation of Hannah.

Anabella (English) A name invented by combining Ana, meaning Grace, and Bella, meaning beautiful. *Annabella*

Anabelle, Anabel (English) A variation of Anabella. *Annabel, Annabelle*

Anahi (Persian) Immortal.

Analia (Spanish) A combination of Ana and Lia.

Anamaria (Spanish) Ana and Maria combined.

Anastasia (Greek) Resurrection. *Anastacia, Stacey, Tasiya*

Anaya (Sanskrit) Free.

Andrea (Scottish) Womanly. *Andra, Andriana, Andy*

Andromeda (Greek) Leader or ruler of men. Mythological status.

Angel (Greek) Angel, messenger.

Angela (Greek) Angel, messenger. *Angelina, Angelica, Angelique*

Anika (Hebrew, Latin, and Sanskrit) Grace.

Anita (Spanish) Grace. A variation of Ann.

Aniya, Aniyah (Russian) Grace. A variation of Ann.

Ann, Anne (English) Grace. A classic name for ever associated with the *Anne of Green Gables* series of books. *Annie*

Analise (German) A combination of Anna and Elise. *Annalise, Annaliese*

Annika (Russian) Grace.

Annora (English) With honour. *Nora, Norah, Onora*

Ansley (Scottish) A meadow. *Ainsley, Ainslee, Ainslie*

Anthea (Greek) Flower.

Antoinette (French) Priceless.

Antonia (Latin) Priceless. A variation of Antoinette.

Anwen (Welsh) Fair, beautiful.

Anya, Aine (Latvian) Grace of God.

Aobh, Aiobh (EE-ve) (Irish) Beautiful, radiant.

Aoibhinn (EE-van) (Irish) Beautiful, radiant.

Aoife (EE-fa) (Irish) Beautiful, radiant.

Aparna (Sanskrit) Leafless.

Apona (Hawaiian) Encompassing.

Apple (English) Nature name famously (or infamously) used by actress Gwyneth Paltrow.

Appolonia (Greek) Feminine form of Apollo, borne by a saint. Meaning unknown.

April (Latin) To open. Sometimes given to girls born in April. *Abril, Avril*

Aqua (Latin) Water. Colour name.

Arabella (Latin) Beautiful altar.

Araceli (Spanish) Altar of heaven.

Araminta (Greek, English) Defender. Derived from the name Amyntas. *Arameta, Minta, Minty*

Arden (Latin) Forest. A unisex Shakespearean name from *As You Like It*.

Arella, Arely (Hebrew) Angel, messenger. A little less direct than Angela.

Aria (Italian) A musical term for an expressive melody.

Ariah (Hebrew) Lion. Used for both boys and girls.

Ariana (Welsh) Silver. *Arianna, Aryanna, Aryana*

Ariel (Hebrew) Lioness of God. *Arielle, Arie, Ariella*

Arista (Greek) Harvest.

Arizona (Spanish) Small spring. A place name that sounds both spirited and soft.

Arlene (English) Pledge.

Arlette (French) Free man. The feminine form of Charles. *Arlet*

Armani (Persian) Desire. A unisex name with high fashion flair.

Arwen (Welsh) Noble maiden. A name we associate with the Princess of the Elves from *The Lord of the Rings*.

Arya (Sanskrit) Noble, truthful.

Ashanti (African)
The name of a region in
western Africa.

Ashley (English) Ash tree.
No longer exclusively a
boy's name.

Ashlyn, Ashlynn
(English) Ash tree. This
name is picking up where
Ashley left off in the 1980s
and 1990s.

Ashton (English)
Ash tree. The actor
Ashton Kutcher took this
name into boy's territory,
but not completely.

Asia (English) Name of
the continent.

Aspen (English) Tree.
This is a unisex nature
and place name, inspired
by the city in Colorado.

Astrid (Scandinavian)
God-like beauty. An
intriguing, elegant name.

Athena (Greek) Goddess
of wisdom.

Atlanta (English) Name
of the city in Georgia.

Aubrey (English) Elf ruler.
This pretty name is
reaching new heights in
popularity. *Aubree*, *Aubri*,
Aubrie

Aubrianna (English) Elf
ruler. Variation of Aubrey.

Auburn (English) Golden
reddish-brown. A colour
name that Amber didn't
even see coming.

Audra (English) Noble
strength. Variation of
Audrey.

Audrey (English) Noble
strength. Made even more
glamorous by the late
Audrey Hepburn. *Audrina*

Audriana (English)
Noble strength. Variation
of Audrey. *Audrianna*

Augusta (Latin) Majestic.
The feminine form of
Augustus.

Augustine (Latin)
Majestic. A softer
variation of Augusta.
Augustina, Agustina

Aurelia (ah-RAIL-ee-uh)
(English) Gold or golden.
Auriol

Aurelie (English) Gold.
A variation of Aurelia.
Oralie, Aurelle

Aurora (Latin) Dawn.
Reminds us of the fairy-
tale Sleeping Beauty and
the Northern Lights.

Austria (German)
Country in central Europe.

Autumn (American)
The fall season.

Ava (Latin) Bird-like.
One of the top 10 most
popular names in America
in recent years.

Avalon (Celtic)
Island of apples.

Avani (Hindu) Earth.

Avery (English) Ruler of elves. *Averi, Averie*

Aviana (Latin) Bird-like. A variation of Ava.

Aviva (Hebrew) Spring.

Ayanna A modern invented name, most likely created as a variation of Anna.

Ayla (Hebrew) Mighty oak tree. *Aila*

Ayleen (Irish) Light. Gaelic variation of Helen. Increasingly popular.

Aylin (EY-lin) (Turkish) Moonlight, halo around the moon. A popular girl's name in Turkey.

Azalea (Latin) Flower. An unusual and unexpected nature name. *Azalia*

Azaria (Hebrew) Helped by God.

Aziza (Hebrew) Strong.

Azriela (Hebrew) God is my strength.

Azura (French) Blue.

A baby is a little bit of heaven on earth.

UNKNOWN

Baha (Arabic) Splendor, glory.

Bailey (English) Bailiff. Recently given a boost thanks to singer Corinne Bailey Rae. *Bailee*, *Baylee*

Bambi (Italian) Child. Delicate and doe-eyed.

Barbara (Greek) Foreign woman. This name was fashionable in the 1950s, but has since faded. *Babb*, *Babbette*, *Babs*, *Barb*, *Barbie*

Basanti (Sanskrit) Spring.

Bay (English) Sea inlet. A unisex nature name.

Beatrice (Latin) She brings joy. *Bea*, *Beatrix*

Beatrix (Latin) She brings joy. A variation of Beatrice discovering new life.

Belen (bel-LEN) (Spanish) Bethlehem. Fitting for a girl born in the Christmas season.

Belinda (English) Dragon. A familiar name with a surprising meaning.

Belize The name of the country in the Caribbean.

Bella, Belle (French) Beautiful.

Bellamy (French) Fair friend.

Benita (Latin) God has blessed.

Bentley (English) Meadow of grass. Also, a luxurious automobile.

Berkeley (English) Birch-tree meadow.

Berlin Place name. The capital of Germany.

Bernadette (French) Brave as a bear. Catholic saint name and a character in the popular TV show *The Big Bang Theory*. *Bernadina, Bernetta, Bernie, Bernita*

Beth (Hebrew) God is my oath. A variation of Elizabeth.

Bethan (Welsh) God is my oath. This variation of Elizabeth is particularly popular in Wales.

Bethany (Hebrew) House of figs. *Bethanie, Bethenny*

Bethel (Hebrew) House of God. A biblical place name with a pleasing twist on Beth.

Beverly (English) Beaver stream.

Bevin (Scottish) Sweet singer. Anglicized form of the Gaelic Bébhinn.

Bianca (Italian) White.

Billie (English) Constant protector. One of the feminine forms of William.

Blaine (Irish) Slender.

Blair (English) A flat piece of land.

Blaise (English) One who stutters. A traditionally male name sometimes used for girls.

Blake (English) Fair-haired, and dark.

Blakely (English) Fair-haired, and dark. A variation of Blake and surname.

Blanca (Spanish) White.

Blanche (English) White.

Blessing Word name usually chosen as a middle name.

Blossom (English) Flower.

Blue (English) Colour name. A recent favourite with celebrities.

Blythe (English) Happy.

Bolivia Place name that puts a spin on Olivia.

Bonnie (Scottish) Beautiful, cheerful.

Braelynn, Braelyn A newly invented name.

Bramley An apple variety with naming potential.

Brandy (Dutch) Burnt wine.

Braylee A newly invented name similar to the English name Brayden.

Breanna (English) Raven. A variation of Brenna.

Bree A feminine form of Brian, Bree is a trendy name meaning brave.

Brenda (Scandinavian) Of old Norse origin. Sword.

Brenna (English) Raven.

Bria (English) Raven.

Brianna (English) Raven. *Briana, Bryanna*

Briar (English) A thorny patch. The original name of the Sleeping Beauty.

Bridget (Irish) Strength. *Brigid, Bridie, Brigitta*

Brielle, Briella (English) Raven. Sometimes a short form of Gabrielle.

Brighton (English) Bright town. A place name referring to the coastal town in England.

Brinkley (English) Bianca's field. A common surname.

Brinley (English) Burnt meadow. *Brynlee*

Briony, Bryony (Latin) To sprout. Also a plant name.

Brisa (Spanish) Breeze.

Bristol (English) Meeting by the bridge. A city in England.

Britton (English) From Britain.

Brittany (English) From Britain. *Britney, Brittan*

Brontë (Greek) Thunder. A name with a literary feel, thanks to the Brontë sisters.

Bronwen (Welsh) Fair breast.

Brooke (English) Small stream.

Brooklyn A place name gaining in popularity due to its similarity to Brooke. *Brooklynn*

Brylee A modern invented name combining Bree with Riley. *Bryleigh*

Brynn (Welsh) Hill. *Bryn, Brynlee, Brinley*

Butterfly (English) A nature name with a bit of a hippie reputation.

C

Cadence (Latin) Rhythm. A musical term with an appropriately lovely sound.

Cadi, Cady (English) A surname with an unknown definition.

Cailyn (Scottish) Triumphant people.

Caitlin (Irish) Pure. A variation of Catherine. *Caitlyn, Catlin, Kaitlin, Katelin, Katelynn*

Calandra (Greek) Lark.

Caledonia (Latin) Scotland. Made famous by Dougie MacLean's folk ballad 'Caledonia'.

Calla (Greek) Lily.

Callie (Greek) Beautiful, lovely. *Cali, Caleigh*

Calliope (Greek) Pretty muse.

Calista (Greek) Beautiful. *Cala, Calissa, Calista, Callie, Callista*

Cambria (Latin) The classical name for Wales.

Cameron (Scottish) Crooked one. A newly unisex name still more popular for boys. *Cam, Camryn, Camira*

Camila (Latin) Church attendant. *Cami, Camilla, Camille, Cammy*

Campbell (Scottish) Crooked mouth.

Cana A biblical town where Jesus turned water into wine.

Candace (English) Pure, sincere. *Candice, Candy*

Caoimhe (KWEE-va) (Irish) Beautiful. A popular name in Ireland.

Capella (Latin) Little goat. One of the brightest stars in the sky.

Caprice (Italian) On a whim, change of mind.

Cara (Italian) Dear. *Caralisa, Carra, Kara*

Carina (Italian) Darling one.

Carissa (Greek) Refined.

Carla (Italian) Woman. A feminine form of Carl. *Karla*

Carlie (Italian) Woman. A contemporary variation of Carla. *Carley, Carlee, Carleigh, Carly*

Carmela (Hebrew) Garden. *Carmella*

Carmen (Hebrew) Garden. The Spanish form of Carmela. *Carmelia*

Carol (German) Woman. This name was at its most popular in the 1950s. *Carole, Caryl*

Carolina (German) Woman. A southern place name.

Caroline (German) Woman. A feminine version of Carl. *Carolyn*

Carrie (German) Woman. A diminutive of Caroline that became popular in the late 1970s.

Carys (CARE-iss) (Welsh) Love. Chosen for their daughter by Catherine Zeta-Jones and Michael Douglas. *Cerys*

Casey (Irish) Vigilant in war. A unisex name. *Cacia, Casie, Kasey*

Cassandra (Greek) She who entangles men. A Shakespearean and Greek mythology name. *Cass, Casson, Kassandra*

Cassia (Greek) Cinnamon. A pretty name with a sweet meaning.

Cassidy (Irish) Curly-haired. *Kassidy*

Cassie (Greek) She who entangles men. A diminutive of Cassandra.

Catalina (Spanish) Pure.

Catarina (Italian) Pure.

Catherine (Greek) Pure. A classic name with a long history of use. *Caitlyn, Cassie, Catey, Cate, Cathleen, Cathryn*

Cátia (Greek) Pure.

Catriona (Greek) Pure. A Gaelic form of Catherine. *Catrina*

Cayenne (French) The spice.

Caylee (Irish) Fair. *Cailee, Cayla*

Cecilia, Celia (Latin) Blind. The feminine version of Cecil. *Cecia, Celina, Cella, Cecy*

Cecily (Latin) Blind. A diminutive of Cecilia.

Ceinwen (Welsh) Blessed fair one. *Cainwen*

Celeste (Latin) Heaven. *Celestia*

Celina (Latin) Heaven.

Céline (French) Heaven. Singer Céline Dion made this name internationally famous.

Cerelia (Latin) Relating to Spring. An unusual seasonal name.

Cerella (English) Springtime.

Cerise (French) Cherry.

Cézanne (French) A name for your little artist, inspired by Impressionist painter Paul Cézanne.

Chana (Hebrew) Grace, God's favour. A variation of Hannah.

Chanel (French) Canal. Associated with French designer Coco Chanel.

Chantal (French) Rocky area.

Charis (CARR-is) (Greek) Grace. The Greek form of Carys.

Charisma (English) Magnetism. A word name originally derived from Charis.

Charity (Latin) A virtue name.

Charley (English) Free. Diminutive of Charles and Charlotte. *Charli, Charlie, Charlee, Charleigh*

Charlize (English) Free. A variation of Charlotte.

Charlotte (English) Free. A classic name that has its roots in the male name Charles. *Carlie, Carline, Char*

Chastity (Latin) Pure, chaste. A virtue name favoured by Puritans in the 1800s. *Chasity*

Chaya (Hebrew) Life.

Chelsea (English) Ship port. A well-liked place name that was at its height in the early 1990s. *Chelsey*

Cher (French) Beloved. No last name necessary.

Cherish (English) To treasure. A sugary-sweet word name.

Cheryl (English) Charity.

Chesney (French) Oak grove.

Cheyenne (Native American) Foreign speakers. A tribal name and place name. *Cheyanne, Shyanne*

China (English) The country. *Chyna*

Chloe (Greek) Young blade of grass.

Christabel (Latin) Beautiful Christian.

Christine (Latin) Anointed, Christian. *Christa, Christie, Cristina, Christina*

Chun (Chinese) Spring.

Ciara (KEER-ah) (Irish) Black.

Cipriana (Greek) From Cyprus.

Cielo (Spanish) Sky.

Claire (French) Bright. The French variation of Clara. *Clare*

Clara (Latin) Bright.

Clarissa (Italian) Bright. The Italian variation of Clara.

Claudia (French) Lame. The feminine form of Claude. *Claudine, Claudie*

Clementine (English) Gentle. A name that may well inspire the singing of a well-known western folk ballad.

Cleopatra (Greek) Her father's pride. Name of the last pharaoh of ancient Egypt. *Cleo*

Clodagh (KLO-da) (Irish) The name of a river in Ireland.

Clover (English) Plant name. A traditional symbol of luck.

Coco (French) People of victory. Favoured by today's celebrities and the late Coco Chanel.

Coda A unisex name and musical term for the end section of a song.

Colette (French) Triumphant people.

Colleen (Gaelic) Girl.

Constance (English) Steady. *Connie, Constanta, Constanza*

Cora (Greek) Maiden.

Coral (English) A nature name for ocean lovers.

Coralie (French) Coral. *Coraline*

Cordelia (English) Heart.

Coretta (Greek) Maiden. The name of Dr. Martin Luther King Jr.'s widow.

Corinne (French) The hollow. *Corina, Corinna*

Corliss (English) Carefree.

Cosette (French) Little thing. Romantic lead in the musical *Les Misérables*.

Cosima (Greek) Order, harmony. The feminine version of Cosmo.

Courtney (English) Dweller in the court. *Courtnie, Kourtney*

Cressida (Greek) Gold.

Crimson (English) Red. A colour name that's less popular than its counterpart, Scarlet.

Crystal (Greek) Ice, Gem. *Christal, Krystal*

Cynthia (Greek) Goddess of the moon. *Cindy*

Cypress (Greek) A tree and an island country in the Mediterranean.

Cyra (Persian) Sun.

Cyrene (Greek) Sovereign queen.

D

Daffodil (French) Flower. A nature name that has seen better days. *Daffy*

Dahlia (English) Flower.

Daisy (English) Flower.

Dakota (Native American) Friendly one. A popular place name associated with the west.

Dalia (Hebrew) Branch.

Dallas (English) A place name; the name of towns in Scotland and the U.S.

Damaris (Latin) Calf.

Damita (Spanish) Princess.

Dana (English) From Denmark.

Danae (Greek) The Greek goddess of music and poetry.

Danica, Danika (Norse) Morning star.

Daniela (Italian) God is my judge. *Daniella*

Danielle (English) God is my judge.

Danna An invented name inspired by Danielle.

Daphne (Greek) Laurel tree. A river nymph in Greek mythology.

Darby (Norse) Where deer graze.

Darcy (Irish) Dark one. Surname used in Jane Austen's *Pride and Prejudice*.

Daria (Greek) Luxurious.

Darla (English) Darling.

Darlene (English) Darling.

Davina (Hebrew) Beloved.

Dawn (English) Sunrise. A nature name and homophone of Don.

Dayana (Arabic) Divine.

Deanna (English) Ocean lover.

Deborah (Hebrew) Bee.

December The month. Usually used for girls born in December.

Dee (English) Nickname derived from Deanna and Diana.

Deidre, Dierdre (Irish) Sorrowful.

Delaney (English) From the alder grove.

Delia (Greek) From Delos.

Delicia (Latin) Delight.

Delilah (Hebrew) Desirable. A biblical name that has shed its temptress associations.

Della (German) Noble. A short form of Adelaide.

Delphine (Greek) Woman from Delphi.

Delysia (Latin) Delight. A variant of Delicia.

Demetria (Greek) Follower of Demeter, Greek goddess of the harvest.

Demi (Greek) Follower of Demeter. The short form of Demetria.

Denise (French) Follower of Dionysos.

Desdemona (Greek) Ill-fated. The wife of Othello in Shakespeare's play.

Desirée (French) Desired.

Destiny (French) Fate. *Destinee*

Devany (Irish) Dark-haired.

Devorah (Hebrew) Bee.

Diamond (English) Jewel.

Diana, Diane (Latin) Devine.

Dina (DEE-na) (Hebrew) Judged. (Spanish) Short form of names ending with -dina.

Dinah (Hebrew) God will judge. A strong and simple biblical name.

Divine (Latin) Heavenly.

Dixie (French) Tenth. A term for the deep southern United States.

Diya (Arabic) Splendor, light.

Djuna The novelist Djuna Barnes introduced this name to Americans in the 1960s.

Dolly (Greek) Gift from God. A nickname derived from Dorothy.

Dominique (Latin) Lord.

Donatella (Italian) Gift from God. Name of the iconic fashion designer Donatella Versace.

Donna (Italian) Woman of the home.

Dora (Greek) Gift.

Doreen (Irish) Gloomy, sullen.

Doris (Greek) Gift of the ocean.

Dorothy (Greek) Gift of God. *Dolly, Dot, Dottie*

Dove, Dovie (English) Nature name. A symbol of peace and the Holy Spirit.

Dream (English) Word name.

Drew (Greek) Strong, manly. Taken from the name Andrew.

Drusilla (Latin) Strong. Biblical name rarely used today.

Duffy (Irish) Dark. *Duff*

Dulce, Dulcie, Dulcey (Latin) Sweet.

Dustine (English) Dusty place. Feminine form of Dusty.

Dyani (Native American) Deer.

Dylan (Welsh) Son of the sea.

A loving heart is the truest wisdom.

CHARLES DICKENS

Great one–syllable baby names for girls

These names are in high demand for parents who have a lengthy last name or are looking for a short-and-sweet middle name to balance out a multiple-syllable first name choice.

One-syllable names have typically been dominated by boys, but you will find the girls' names listed here are elegant, sweet, and feminine.

Ann or	Faith	Paige
Anne	Fawn	Pearl
Belle	Grace	Quinn
Bleu or	Hope	Rain or
Blue	Jane	Raine
Bree	June	Rose
Cate or	Kay	Sky or
Kate	Lark	Skye
Claire or	Love	Sloane
Clare	Mae or	Snow
Dove	May	Wynn or
Elle	Maeve	Wynne
Eve	Neve	

Princess names

So many little girls dream of being a princess dressed in a ball gown and wearing a tiara. Whether inspired by a fairy tale or the Duchess of Cambridge, it's a fascination some of us never outgrow. Here are some names that are perfect for the princess in your little girl, inspired by both real-life and fictional royal young ladies.

Adelaide	Charlotte	Máxima
Alexandra	Diana	Sophie
Alice	Estelle	Tiana
Amelia	Fabiola	Victoria
Anne	Giselle	Winifred
Ariel	Helena	
Arwen	Isabella	
Augusta	Isolde	
Aurora	Jasmine	
Belle	Joan	
Cassandra	Letizia	
Catherine	Madeleine	

E

Eabha (AY-vah) (Irish)
Life. The Irish form of Eve.

Eadoin (AY-deen) (Irish)
Blessed with many
friends.

Eartha (English) Earth.
Famously borne by singer
and actress Eartha Kitt.

Easter (English)
The holiday.

Ebony (English)
Dark wood.

Echo (Greek) A nymph
from ancient mythology.

Eden (Hebrew)
Pleasure. Biblical
garden of paradise.

Edith (English)
Prosperity in war.

Edna (Hebrew)
Rejuvenation.

Edwina (English)
Rich friend.

Effie (Greek)
Well-spoken.

Eilah (Hebrew) Oak tree.
Ailah, *Elah*

Eileen (Irish)
Shining, bright.

Eilidh (AY-lee) (Scottish)
Bright.

Eimear (EE-mer) (Gaelic)
Swift.

Eira (AY-ruh) (Welsh)
Snow.

Ekaterina (Greek)
Pure. Slavic variant
of Katherine.

Elaine (French) Bright.
Derivative of Helen,
now associated with the
sitcom *Seinfeld*. *Alaina*,
Elani, *Lainey*

Elara (Greek)
Mythological name
and one of the moons
of Jupiter.

Eleanor, Eleanora
(English) Mercy.

Electa (Greek) Elect.
Derived from a passage
in the Bible and Masonic
tradition.

Electra (Greek) Bright,
shining. A mythological
figure with a dark past.
Powerful and unusual.

Elaina (Greek) Bright.

Elfreda, Elfrida (English)
Elf power.

Eliana (Hebrew) God has
answered my prayers.
Elianna

Elin (Swedish) Light.
Variation of Ellen.

Elisha (Hebrew) God
is my salvation. A male
biblical name sometimes
used for girls.

Elizabeth (Hebrew)
God is my oath. A classic
name with countless
variations. *Beth*, *Bethan*,
Buffy, *Elisabeth*, *Elsa*,
Elisa, *Eliza*, *Elise*, *Elsie*,
Elspeth, *Isabel*, *Libby*,
Lizzy, *Zizi*

Ella (German) Completely,
all. (Spanish) Young girl.
(Latin) Light. *Ellie*

Elle (German) All.
See Ella. A pretty and
to-the-point variation.

Ellen (English) Light.
Elen, *Elena*

Ellery (English)
Island with elder trees.

Elliot (English)
God on high.

Ellison (English)
Son of Ellis.

girls

Elodie (French) Flower.

Eloise (French) Wise.

Elowen (Cornish) Elm.

Elsa (Spanish) Noble.

Eluned (Welsh) Idol.

Elvira (Spanish) White, fair.

Elyse (Latin) Light.

Ember (English) Spark, burning coal.

Emelia (German) Industrious. A variation of Amelia.

Emer (Gaelic) Swift.

Emerald (English) Green gem.

Emerson (German) Son of the chief. *Emersyn*

Emery (German) Leader of the house.

Emese (EM-esh-eh) (Hungarian) Mother.

Emily (English) Industrious. A classic name that's often in the American top 10. *Emilie, Emilee, Emely, Emmalee, Emmeline, Milly*

Emina (Latin) Beloved.

Emma (German) All, total. *Emmalyn, Emmy*

Emory (English) Home strength.

Ena (Irish) Bright.

Enya, Eithne (Irish) Fire.

Erica (Scandanavian) Eternal leader. *Erika*

Erin (Irish) From the island. Also an alternative name for Ireland.

Erma (German) All, total.

Ernestine (English) Serious. The feminine form of Ernest.

Errolyn Unknown meaning. Errolyn is popular in Australia.

Esmé (French) Esteemed.

Esmeralda (Spanish) Emerald.

Esperanza (Spanish) Hope.

Essence (English) True nature, perfume.

Estelle, Estella (French) Star.

Esther (Persian) Star.

Estrella (English) Child of the stars.

Eternity (English) A word name with beautiful connotations.

Ethel (English) Noble.

Etta (English) A feminine suffix. This pretty name has jazzy overtones.

Eugenie (Greek) Well born. Chosen by the Duke and Duchess of York for their daughter. *Eugenia*

Eunice (Greek) Victorious.

Eustacia (Greek) Fruitful.

Eva, Efa (Hebrew) Giver of life. Eva is rising in popularity in the U.S.

Evangeline (Greek) Good news.

Evanthe (Greek) Fair flower.

Evanthia (Greek) Fair flower. *Eva, Thea*

Eve, Evie (Hebrew) Life. Biblical name of the first woman.

Evelyn (French) Hazelnut. Today, this name is experiencing new life. *Evelynn, Evlyn*

Ever (English) Word name with modern appeal.

Everly (English) From the boar meadow. An appealing choice in the vein of Emily and Eva.

Ezra (Hebrew) Helper. A biblical male name sometimes used for girls.

The best gift in life is to hold a new one in your arms.

ANONYMOUS

Fabienne (French)
One who grows beans.
The feminine form of
Fabian. *Fabiola*

Fable (English) A story
conveying a moral. An
unexpected word name.

Faida (Arabic) Abundant.

Faith (English) A virtue
name.

Farrah (English) Pleasant.
Made famous by the late
actress Farrah Fawcett.

Fatima (Arabic) Nurse.
The name of Muhammad's
favourite daughter.

Fawn (French) Young deer.

Fay, Faye (French) Fairy.

Felicity (Latin) Happy.
Felicia

Fenella, Finola (Celtic)
White-haired one.

Fergie (Scottish) Best
choice. Nickname of the
Duchess of York and the
Black Eyed Peas singer.

Fern (English) Valley of
ferns. *Ferne, Fernley*

Fernanda (German)
Peace and courage.

Ffion, Fionn (Welsh)
Foxglove.

Fiala (Czech) Violet.

Fiamma (Italian) Flame.

Fianna (Irish) Fair, white.

Fifi (French) God will
increase. Diminutive of
Josephine.

Finley (Irish) Fair-haired
hero.

Filia (Greek) Friendship.

Finola (Irish)
White shoulders.

Fiona (Gaelic) Fair, white.
Popularized by a Scottish
poet in the early 20th
century.

Fiora (Gaelic) Fair, white.

Fiorella (Italian)
Little flower.

Flavia (Latin) Golden,
blonde.

Fleur (French) Flower.

Flora (Latin) Flower.
The name of the Roman
goddess of springtime

Florence (Latin) Blooming,
flower. Place name that hit
its peak in the early 1900s
and is popular again today,
especially in the UK.

Floriana (Latin) Flower.

France A place name.

Frances (English) One
who is from France. *Fran,
Francesca, Francine*

Frederica, Freda
(German) Merciful leader.

Freesia (Latin) Flower.

Freya (Swedish) Noble
lady. Popular in the UK, but
almost unknown in the U.S.

Frida (German)
Peaceful ruler. *Frieda*

Fusi (Polynesian) Bananas.

girls

G

Gabrielle, Gabriella (Hebrew) Heroine of God. *Gabie, Gabrina, Gaby, Gigi, Gabryelle*

Gaia (Greek) Earth.

Gail (Hebrew) My father rejoices. *Gayle*

Gala (Swedish) Celebration.

Galilea (Italian) From Galilee.

Galina (Russian) Bright, shining one.

Gardenia (English) Flower.

Garland (French) Wreath.

Garnet (English) Jewel.

Geena (Hebrew) Garden. Variation of Gina borne by actress Geena Davis.

Gemma (Irish) Jewel.

Genesis (Hebrew) Beginning. A biblical name catching on with creative parents.

Geneva (French) Juniper tree. Name of a picturesque city in Switzerland.

Genevieve (Celtic) White.

Georgette (Latin) Farmer. Variation of George. *Georgiana, Georgina*

Georgia (Latin) Farmer. Feminine form of George and southern place name.

Geraldine (French) Ruler with a spear.

Germaine (French) One from Germany.

Gertrude (German) Ruler with a spear. *Gertie, Trudy*

Gia (Italian) Queen.

Giada (Italian) Jade.

Gianna (Italian) God is good. *Giana*

Gigi French nickname, possibly derived from Georgina.

Gillian (English) Youthful.

Gina (Hebrew) Garden.

Ginger (English) The spice.

Gioia (JOY-a) (Italian) Joy.

Giordana (Italian) River. The Italian form of Jordana.

Giovanna (Italian) God is good.

Giselle (English) Oath. Perfect for a ballerina.

Gitana (Spanish) Gypsy.

Giuliana (Italian) Young. The Italian variation of Juliana.

Gladiola (Latin) Sword. The feminine form of Gladiolus and the name of a flower.

Gladys (Welsh) Lame. A form of Claudia that was once considered very stylish.

Glenda (Welsh) Holy and good.

Glenna (Irish) Narrow valley.

Glenys (Welsh) Holy.

Glimmer (English) Word name used in the novel *The Hunger Games*.

Gloria (Latin) Glory. A lovely name that enjoyed its best days in the 1920s.

Glory (Latin) A variation of Gloria.

Goldie Anglicized form of the Yiddish Golde, Golda.

Grace (Latin) Grace. A virtue name that became a stylish classic. *Gracie*

Gracelynn, Gracelyn (Latin) Grace. A newly created and increasingly popular variation of the eternally popular Grace.

Grainne, Grania (Irish) Goddess of grain.

Greta (German) Pearl. Variation of Margaret.

Gretchen (German) Pearl.

Guadalupe (Spanish) Valley of wolves. *Lupe*

Guinevere (Welsh) White wave. *Genevive, Genna, Gwen, Ginevra, Winnie*

Gwendolyn, Gwen (Welsh) Fair brow. *Gwen*

Gwyneth (Welsh) Happiness. *Gwynne, Gwynnie, Wynnie*

Gypsy (English) Wanderer. *Gypsie*

H

Hadassah (Hebrew) Myrtle tree.

Hadley (English) Meadow of heather. *Hadlee, Hadleigh*

Hailey (English) Hay field. Very popular in the US, with spelling variations galore. *Hailee, Haleigh, Haley, Haylee, Hayleigh, Hayley, Haylie*

Halle (Scandinavian) Heroine. *Hallie*

Halona (Native American) Good luck.

Hannah (Hebrew) Grace. Popular biblical name and palindrome. *Hanna*, *Hana*

Harley (English) Rabbit pasture. A delicate name with a motorcycle edge. *Harleigh*, *Harlie*

Harlow (English) Army. Used by designer Nicole Richie for her daughter.

Harmony (Latin) Harmonious, in concord.

Harper (English) Harp player. Literary name gaining favour in the US.

Harriet (German) Leader of the house. *Henrietta*

Hattie Variation of Harriet. So old-fashioned it's cool again.

Haulani (Hawaiian) Royalty.

Haven (English) Refuge. Rarer than Hailey, subtler than Heaven.

Hayden (English) Heather-covered hill. Unisex name and a common surname.

Hazel (English) Hazelnut tree.

Heather (English) Flower.

Heaven, Heavenly (English) Paradise.

Heidi (German) Noble.

Helen (Greek) Light. A historic name with a multitude of spin-offs. *Aileen*, *Alena*, *Elaine*, *Elena*, *Ellen*, *Helena*, *Ilona*, *Lena*, *Olena*, *Yelena*

Héloïse (French) Famous in war.

Henley (English) High meadow. Also, the name of a place and a T-shirt.

Henrietta (German) Ruler of the home. The feminine form of Henry.

Hermione (Greek) Messenger. Female star of the Harry Potter series.

Hesper (Greek) Evening star.

Hibiscus (Latin) Flower.

Hilary, Hillary (Greek) Glad.

Hilda (German) Battle woman.

Holiday (English) Word name with a carefree, celebratory feel.

Holland Dutch place name.

Holly (English) Plant.

Honesty (English) A Puritanical virtue name.

Honey (English) Word name.

Honour (English) A virtue name. *Honora*, *Honoria*

Hope (English) A popular virtue name.

Horatia (English) A Roman clan name.

Hosanna (Greek) A prayer of praise.

Hyacinth (Greek) Flower.

I

Ianthe (Greek) Flower.

Ida (English) Youth.

Idele (German) Youth.

Idina (English) From Edinburgh, Scotland. Made known by the actress Idina Menzel.

Idonia (Norse) Renewal. The Spanish form of Idony.

Ignacia (Latin) On fire. The feminine form of Ignatius.

Ila, Ilia (English) From Troy.

Ilana (Hebrew) Oak tree.

Ilene (Greek) Light. A variation of Helen.

Iliana (Greek) From Troy.

Ilona (Hungarian) Pretty.

Ilsa (Scottish) God is my oath. A variation of Elizabeth.

Imala (Native American) Discipline.

Imani (Arabic) Faith.

Imena (African) Dream.

Imogen (Celtic) Maiden, innocent.

India (English) Stylish and exotic place name.

Indiana (English) Place name made more famous by the *Indiana Jones* films.

Indra (Sanskrit) Beauty.

Ineka (Hebrew) Gracious.

Ines, Inez (Spanish) Pure. The Spanish and French variations of Agnes.

Ingrid, Inga (Scandinavian) Beautiful.

Iola (Greek) Violet.

Iolanthe (yo-LAN-thuh) (Greek) Violet flower. *Yolanda, Yola*

Iona (Scottish) Island in Scotland.

Ireland (English) The country.

Irene (Greek) Peace.

Irina (Greek) Peace. A variation of Irene.

Iris (Greek) Rainbow. A flower and the Greek goddess of the rainbow.

Irish (English) From Ireland.

Isabeau (Spanish) God is my oath.

Isabel (Spanish) God is my oath. *Isabelle, Isobel*

Isabella (Spanish) God is my oath. A top-ten star in the US. *Isabela, Izabella*

Isadora (Latin) Gift of Isis. A pretty and unusual name with a sound similar to Isabella.

Iset (Egyptian) Goddess.

Ishana (Hindu) Desire.

Ishara (Hindu) Rich.

Ishi (Japanese) Stone.

Isis (Egyptian) Goddess.

Isla (EYE-la) (Scottish) The name of a river in Scotland.

Isolde (Welsh) Fair lady.

Isotta (Welsh) Fair lady. A variant of Isolde.

Israel, Israella (Hebrew) God preserves.

Italia (Latin) From Italy. *Italy, Italya*

Itinsa (Native American) Waterfall.

Itzel (Spanish) Star.

Ivana (Slavic) God is good. *Ivanna, Ivanka*

Ivara (German) Yew tree.

Ivette (French) Arrow's bow.

Ivonne (French) Yew wood.

Ivory (Latin) Ivory.

Ivy (English) Plant. A charming nature name.

Jacey A modern invented name derived from the initials J.C. *Jaycee*

Jacinta (Spanish) Hyacinth.

Jacoba (Hebrew) Supplanter, heel. The feminine form of Jacob.

Jacqueline (French) He who replaces. *Jackalyn, Jackie, Jacqui*

Jada (American) Precious stone. *Jaida, Jayda*

Jade (Spanish) Precious stone. *Jayde*

Jaden (Hebrew) Thankful. A modern name created from Jade. *Jadyn, Jaiden, Jaidyn, Jayden*

Jaelyn A modern invented name. *Jaelynn, Jaelyn, Jaylin, Jaylyn, Jaylynn*

Jaio (Chinese) Pretty, gentle.

Jakayla A modern invented name.

Jala (Arabic) Great.

Jamaica Place name; the West Indies island.

Jamie (English) One who replaces.

Janae (Hebrew) God answers.

Jane (English) God's grace. A simple and sweet classic name. *Jayne, Jean*

Janelle (English) God's grace. A modern variation of Jane.

Janessa (American) A combination of Jan and Vanessa.

Janet (English) God's grace. A diminutive of Jane that was very popular in the 1960s.

Janice, Janis (English) God's grace.

Janine (English) God is good. *Jeanette, Jeannine*

Janiya A modern invented name. *Janiyah*

Jasmine (Persian) The flower. A beautiful name thrown into the spotlight by Aladdin. *Jasmin, Jessamy, Jazmine, Jazmin, Yasmin*

Jayla, Jaylah (American) A created name combining Jada and Kayla.

Jayleen, Jaylene (English) Blue jay.

Jazlyn (American) A combination of Jazz and Lynn. *Jaslene, Jazlene, Jazlynn*

Jean (Scottish) God is good. A feminine form of John. *Jeana, Jeanna, Jeanne, Jennette*

Jelena (Russian) Light. A variation of Helen.

Jem (English) Supplanter. A feminine form of James.

Jemima (Hebrew) Dove. Popular in the UK, where it's a chic choice. *Jemimah, Jemmie, Mima*

Jemma (English) Precious stone. A variation of Gemma.

Jennifer (Welsh) White wave. This name was wildly popular in the 1970s. *Jenny, Jenna, Jen*

Jersey (English) A place name that sounds bright and breezy.

Jessica (Hebrew) God sees. A Shakespearean name that has remained popular since the 1980s. *Jessie, Jess*

Jetta (English) Jet. *Jet, Jeta, Jettie*

Jewel (French) Gem-like. *Jewell, Jewelle*

Jill (English) Young.

Jillian (English) Young. *Gillian, Gillie, Jilian, Jilana*

Jimena (Spanish) Heard.

Jin (Japanese) Excellent.

Jiya (Tamil) Sweet.

Joan (Hebrew) God is good. An ancient name with a rich history. *Joanie, Joanee, Joni, Sion* (Welsh)

Joanna (English) God is good. *Jana, Jo, JoAnn, Johanna*

Joanne (French) God is good. The French form of Joanna.

Jocasta (Greek) Happy. Used more often in the UK than in the US, by no fault of its own.

Jocelyn (German) Member of the ancient German Gauts tribe. *Jocelynn, Joselyn, Joslyn, Joscelin*

Jodi (Hebrew) Praised.

Joelle (Hebrew) God is Lord. The feminine form of Joel.

Jola (Greek) Violet flower.

Jolanta (Czech) Violet flower.

Jolana (American) A variant of Jo.

Jolene A modern invented name, made famous in a song by Dolly Parton.

Jolie (French) Pretty. *Jolee, Joleigh, Joli*

Jonella (English) God is good.

Jora (Hebrew) Autumn rain.

Jordan (English) To descend. *Jordyn, Jordynn*

Jorina (Hebrew) Flowing down.

Josephine (Hebrew) God will add. A historic name with a classy feel. *Josie, Fifi, Josetta, Jo*

Journey A word name that is slowly climbing the charts in popularity. *Journee*

Joy A cheerful name with holiday overtones.

Joyce (Latin) Joyous.

Juanita (Spanish) God is good.

Jubilee (Hebrew) Ram's horn.

Judith (Hebrew) Woman from Judea. A classic biblical name.

Judy (Hebrew) Woman from Judea. A variant of Judith with 1940s style.

Julene (Latin) Jove's descendant.

Julia, Julie (English) Young, youthful. Eternally popular around the world, Julia is a classic. *Juley, Juliana, Julissa, Yula*

Julianne (Latin) Youthful. *Juliana, Julianna*

Juliet (English) Downy. This romantic variant of Julia is currently enjoying a revival in popularity. *Julietta, Juliette, Julieta*

Julissa An invented name combining the charms of Julia and Alissa.

June (Latin) The month. The vintage sound of this name is hitting a sweet spot with parents today.

Juneau A place name referring to the capital of Alaska.

Junia A Roman clan name. This is the feminine form of Junius, and a biblical name.

Juniper (English) The evergreen shrub.

Juno (Latin) Queen of heaven. Recently brought to our attention by the 2007 indie film of the same name.

Justice A virtue name used more often for boys.

Justine (French) Just. *Justina*

Kacey (Irish) Vigilant in war. Variant of Casey.

Kadence (Latin) Rhythm. Variant of Cadence. *Kaydence*

Kaelyn (Scottish) Triumphant people. A variant of Cailyn. *Kaelynn, Kailyn, Kailynn, Kaylen, Kaylin*

Kai (Hawaiian) Sea. A unisex name that is currently more popular for boys.

Kaia (Greek) Earth.

Kailey (Hebrew) Laurel, crown. A variant of Kayla. *Kailee, Kaleigh, Kaylee, Kaylee, Kayleigh, Kaylie*

Kairi (KY-ree) (Japanese) Sea.

Kaisa (Swedish) Pure.

Kaitlin (Irish) Pure. *Kaitlyn, Kaitlynn*

Kaiya (Japanese) Forgiveness.

Kalani (Hawaiian) Heaven.

Kalila (Arabic) Beloved. A common term of endearment in Arabic countries.

Kalinda (Hindi) Sun.

Kaliyah (Arabic) Beloved. Variant of Kalila.

Kallie (Greek) Beautiful, lovely.

Kamala (Hindu) Lotus.

Kamara (American) An invented name.

Kamila (French) Church attendant. Variant of Camila.

Kamille (French) Church attendant. Variant of Camille.

Kamryn (Scottish) Crooked one. A variant of Cameron.

Kara (Latin) Dear. A variant of Cara that has usurped its predecessor.

Karen (Greek) Pure. *Karin*, *Karina*

Karenza (Cornish) Love. *Kerensa*

Karissa (Italian) Darling one.

Karlie (Italian) Woman. An updated form of Carla. *Karlee*, *Karly*

Karma (Hindu) Fate.

Karsyn (English) Son of the swamp-dwellers. Feminine form of Carson.

Katarina (Greek) Pure. A variation of Katherine with an international feel. *Katerina*, *Katrine*

Katelyn (Irish) Pure. *Katelynn*

Katherine (Greek) Pure. One of the most long-standing and popular names of all time. *Katalina*, *Katriona*, *Kathryn*, *Kate*, *Kitty*

Kathleen (Irish) Pure.

Katie (Greek) Pure. A girl-next-door diminutive of Katherine.

Katrina (Greek) Pure.

Katya (Russian) Pure.

Kay, Kaye (English) Pure. A one-syllable variation of Katherine.

Kaya (Native American) Older sister.

Kayden (Irish) A form of Cadan, which means son of Cadán.

Kayla (English) Pure.

Keara (Irish) Dark.

Keely (Gaelic) Slender, pretty.

Keira, Kiera (Irish) Dark. Catapulted to popularity by actress Keira Knightley.

Keisha An invented name likely inspired by the Hebrew Kezia, meaning Cassia tree.

K

Kelly (Irish) Soldier. Transitioned from a surname to a boys' name to girls' territory.

Kelsey (English) Island. *Kelsie*, *Kelsea*, *Kelsi*

Kendal (English) The valley of the Kent river in Cumbria. *Kendall*, *Kendyl*

Kendra Likely a form of Kenneth, meaning beautiful, born of fire.

Kenley (English) The king's meadow.

Kenna (Irish) Beautiful, born of fire. A feminine form of Kenneth.

Kennedy (Irish) Misshapen head. A name that evokes all-American glamour. *Kennedi*

Kensley (Gaelic) Descendant of ancient Irish chieftan Cinnsealach.

Kenya An African place name.

Kenzie (Scottish) Fair skinned.

Kerry (German) Woman. Alternative spelling of Carrie. *Keri*

Ketina (Hebrew) Girl.

Kezia (Hebrew) Cassia tree.

Khloe (Greek) Young blade of grass. Alternative spelling of Chloe, recently growing more popular.

Kiana An American name with debated meaning.

Kiara (Latin) Light, clear. Also cited as having Irish origins, meaning dark.

Kiersten (Scandinavian) Anointed. *Kirsten*, *Kirstie*

Kimberly (English) Royal meadow. *Kim*, *Kimber*

Kimora A combination of names Kim and Ora.

Kinley (Irish) Fair-haired hero. *Kynlee*

Kinsey (English) King's victory. A name easily imagined for a little girl.

Kinsley (English) King's meadow.

Kira (Greek) Lady.

Kirsten, Kirstie (Scandinavian) Anointed.

Kizzy (Hebrew) Cassia tree. A long history of use in Africa, as seen in the book *Roots* by Alex Haley.

Kristen (English) Anointed. *Krissy*, *Kristene*, *Krysia*

Kyla (Hebrew) Crown. *Kylah*

Kylie (Australian Aboriginal) Boomerang. *Kiley*, *Kylee*, *Kyleigh*

Kyndall (English) The Kent river valley. Variant of Kendall. *Kyndal*

Kyra (Greek) Lady.

Kyrie (Irish) Dark.

Lacey (French) From the old French name Laci.

Lady (English) Noble title.

Laila, Lailah (Arabic) Dark beauty. *Layla.*

Laine (English) Bright one. *Lane*

Lainey, Laney (English) Bright one.

Lakota (Native American) Friend to us. Dakota alternative.

Lalana (Sanskrit) Playing.

Lana (English) Rock.

Langley (English) A surname meaning long meadow.

Lara (Latin) Protection. This name has a variety of origins and is used around the world.

Larissa (Greek) Happy, playful.

Lark A bird known for its song as well as a word meaning a carefree adventure.

Laura (Latin) The laurel plant. A classic name that will always be stylish. *Laurie, Lora*

Laurel (Latin) The laurel plant. A derivative of Laura with the feel of a nature name.

Lauren (Latin) The laurel plant. *Lauryn*

Lavender (English) The herb and colour.

Lavinia (Latin) From Lavinium. Lavinia was a character in Roman mythology and in Shakespeare's *Titus Andronicus*. *Lovinia, Vinnie*

Layla (Arabic) Dark beauty. Revived in Eric Clapton's acoustic rendition in the early 1990s. *Laylah, Leila*

Leah (Hebrew) Weary. *Lea, Lia, Leia, Leigha*

Leandra (Latin) Lion-like.

Leanna (Gaelic) Flowering vine.

Legacy A word name packed with meaning.

Leigh (English) Meadow.

Leighton (English) From the town by the meadow.

Leilani (Hawaiian) Heavenly.

Lena (English) Bright one.

Lenna (German) Strength of a lion.

Lenora (English) Mercy.

Leona (Latin) Lion.

Leonora (English) Mercy.

Leslie, Lesly (Scottish) Garden by the pool.

Leticia (Latin) Joy. *Laetitia*

Leviah (Hebrew) God's lioness.

Lexa (Czech) Protector of man.

Lexi, Lexie (Greek) Man's defender. A variation of Alexandra.

Leya (Spanish) The law.

Liana (French) Twist like a vine.

Libby (Hebrew) God is my oath. A variation of Elizabeth.

Liberty (English) Freedom.

Liesl (German) God is my oath. A variation of Elizabeth.

Lila (Arabic) Night; (Persian) Lilac. *Lilah, Lyla, Lylah*

Lilac (English) The flower.

Lilia (Hawaiian) Lilies.

Liliana (English) Lily. A floral variation becoming popular with parents. *Lilianna, Lilliana, Lillianna, Lilyana, Lilyanna*

Lilith (Arabic) Night demon. An evil figure from Jewish mythology.

Lillian (English) A combination of Lily and Ann. *Lilian, Lillia, Lilyan*

Lily (Latin) Flower. Favoured even more today than it was in the early 1900s. *Lilly, Lillie*

Lina (Arabic) Palm tree.

Linda (Spanish) Pretty one.

Lindsay (English) Island of linden trees. *Lindsey*

Linnea (lin-NAY-a) (Scandinavian) Lime tree. A lovely name that's growing in popularity.

Liora (Hebrew) Light.

Lisa, Lisette (Hebrew) God is my oath.

Lisandra (Greek) Liberator.

Livia, Liv (Latin) Olive tree. Variant of Olivia.

Logan (Scottish)
Little hollow.

Lola (English) Sorrow.

London Place name
that's becoming more
popular in the US.

Lorelei (German)
Temptress. *Lorelai*

Loretta (Latin)
The laurel plant.

Lorna (Scottish) Created
from Lorn, an area in
Scotland.

Lorraine (French)
Provincial place name.

Losaki (Polynesian)
To meet.

Lottie (English) Free.

Louise (English) Female
soldier. *Louisa, Lou*

Louisiana (French)
A place name that
combines the charms
of Louise and Ana.

Lourdes (French)
A place in France with
great significance to those
of the Catholic faith.

Love (English) A virtue
name. *Lovely, Lovey*

Lowri, Lowry (Welsh)
Laurel.

Luana (German)
A combination of Louise
and Anna.

Lucerne (Latin) Lamp.

Lucetta (English) Light.
Lucette

Lucia (Latin) Light.
A name with Scandinavian
and saintly connections.
Lucinda, Luciana

Lucille (French) Light.
This variation of Lucy was
popular in the 1940s and
is now coming back into
fashion. *Lucilla, Lucile*

Lucy (English) Light.

Lula (English) Famous
warrior. A nickname for
Louise.

Lulu (Arabic) Pearl;
(English) Famous warrior.

Luna (Latin) Moon.

Lupita (Spanish) Valley
of wolves. Short form of
Guadalupe.

Luz (Spanish) Light.

Lydia (Greek) Woman
from Lydia. Mentioned in
the Bible as well as *Pride
and Prejudice*.

Lynn (English) Pretty.
Lyn, Lynette

Lyra (Greek) Harp.

Lyric (English) Poetry,
words of a song.

Lyris, Lyra (Greek)
Lyre, harp.

Lysandra (Greek)
Liberator. Feminine form
of Lysander.

The fastest-rising girls' names in England and Wales

These increasingly popular names offer an insightful look into naming trends in England and Wales. As the list shows, hitting all sorts of buttons are names that end in a vowel sound such as 'ia', 'ie', or 'la'. Also favoured are girls names that are floral, nature-inspired or have an old-fashioned appeal.

1	Willow	14	Sienna
2	Bella	15	Emilia
3	Eliza	16	Isla
4	Evelyn	17	Lydia
5	Elsie	18	Alice
6	Kayla	19	Elizabeth
7	Layla	20	Maryam
8	Rose	21	Matilda
9	Harriet	22	Amelia
10	Sophia	23	Eva
11	Lilly	24	Phoebe
12	Annabelle	25	Rosie
13	Florence		

The fastest-rising girls' names in the US

Many of the latest on-trend girls' names in America have their origins in a pop-culture phenomenon, such as a reality TV show or a character in a popular book. Conversely, some names just hit parents with the right sound at the same time. Several of these trendsetting girls' names feature a 'br' sound. Also popular is an 'ley' or 'ee' suffix.

1	Briella	14	Adalynn
2	Angelique	15	Aubrie
3	Aria	16	McKinley
4	Mila	17	Parker
5	Elsie	18	Brynn
6	Nylah	19	Gemma
7	Raelynn	20	Gia
8	Brynlee	21	Nyla
9	Olive	22	Kinsley
10	June	23	Aylin
11	Bristol	24	Willow
12	Aubree	25	Elliana
13	Charlee		

girls

M

Mab (Irish) Joy. English spelling of the Queen of Fairies in Irish legend.

Mabel (English) Loveable.

Mackenzie (Irish) Child of a wise leader. *Makenzie*

Macy (French) Weapon; (English) from the surname Massey. *Macey, Maci*

Mädchen (MADE-chun) (German) Girl, maiden.

Madeline (French) Of Magdala. Brought to life in Ludwig Bemelmans' *Madeline* series. *Madelyn*

Madison (English) Son of a mighty warrior. *Maddison, Madisyn*

Mae (English) Pearl. A pet form of Margaret as well as a form of May.

Maeve (MAY-v) (Irish) Intoxicating. This Irish folklore name is becoming more familiar in the US.

Magdalena (Spanish) From Magdala.

Magnolia (French) Flowering tree. Nature name dripping with southern charm.

Mahogany (Spanish) Dark wood.

Mairéad (muh-RAID) (Irish) Pearl.

Maisie (Scottish) Pearl. A sweet variation of Margaret popular in the UK.

Makenna (Irish) From a surname meaning son of Cionaodh. *McKenna*

Malaya (Sanskrit) Sandalwood tree.

Malaysia A place name.

Maleah (Hawaiian) Perhaps.

Malia (Hawaiian) Defiance. *Maliah, Maliyah*

Mallory (French) Ill-fated. This name hasn't looked back since the 1980s sitcom *Family Ties*.

Manuela (Spanish) God is with us.

Maple Syrupy-sweet word name.

Mara (Hebrew) Bitter.

Marcella (Italian) Warlike. Female form of Marcel. *Marcie*

Marchesa (French) Noblewoman.

Marcia (Latin) Warlike. *Marsha*

Margaret (English) Pearl. This historic name has been cherished for centuries. *Daisy, Greta, Gretchen, Madge, Maisie, Maggie, Marge, May, Meg, Megan, Molly, Peggy, Rita*

Margarita (Spanish) Pearl.

Margot (French) Pearl. *Margaux, Margo*

Maria (Latin) Variation of Mary.

Mariah (Latin) Bitter. Star-powered and fashionable form of Mary.

Mariana (Spanish) Bitter. *Marianna, Marianne*

Maribel (French) Bitter, beautiful. An unexpected French twist on Mary.

M

Marie (French) Bitter.

Mariela (Italian) Bitter.

Marigold (English) A fanciful flower name with a familiar diminutive.

Marilla (Irish) Shining sea. Motherly character in *Anne of Green Gables*.

Marilyn (English) A glamorous combination of Mary and Lynn.

Marina (Latin) From the sea. A fashionable Shakespearean name.

Marion (French) Bitter. *Marian, Marianne*

Mariposa (Spanish) Butterfly.

Maris (Latin) Star of the sea.

Marissa (Latin) Star of the sea. *Marisa*

Marisela (Latin) Star of the sea.

Marisol (Spanish) Bitter sun.

Maritza (Spanish) Star of the sea.

Marjorie (English) Pearl.

Marla (English) Bitter.

Marlene (English) Bitter.

Marley (English) Seaside meadow. Surname of reggae star Bob Marley. *Marlee, Marli*

Marnie (Hebrew) To rejoice. *Marni*

Marta (Italian) Lady.

Martha (Aramaic) Lady.

Martina (Latin) Warlike. Feminine form of Martin. *Martine*

Mary (Hebrew) Bitter. A biblical name that will always remain a classic. *Mari, Mamie, Marabel, Maura, Mitzi, Marietta, Molly, Polly*

Matilda (German) Maiden in battle. Fashionably old-fashioned. *Mattie, Tillie*

Maui Hawaiian place name.

Maureen (Irish) Bitter.

Maxine (Latin) Greatest.

May (English) Pearl. A month name as well as a nickname for Margaret.

Maya (Hindu) God's power. Mythological in both Indian and Greek legends. *Maia, Maja*

Mayra (Irish) Bitter.

Mckenna (Irish) From a surname meaning son of Cionaodh. *Makenna*

Mckenzie (Irish) Child of a wise leader.

Mckinley (Irish) Son of the white warrior.

Meadow A nature name.

Megan (English) Pearl. *Meghan*

Mei (Japanese) Bright, reliant.

Melanie (Greek) Dark-skinned. *Melina*

Melinda (Latin) Honey; sweet. *Lindy*, *Mellinda*

Melissa (Greek) Bee. *Missy*, *Mylissa*

Melita (Greek) Honey.

Melody (Greek) Song.

Memphis Name of the city in Tennessee.

Mercedes (Spanish) Mercy.

Mercy An uncommon virtue name that hasn't returned to favour since Puritan times. *Mercia*

Meredith (Welsh) Great leader. Soft and feminine name enjoying an increase in popularity.

Merrigan (Gaelic) Descendant of the ancient Irish chieftan Muiregán. Surname that sounds like a combination of Mary and Megan.

Meryl (English) Bright as the sea. Linked with the actress Meryl Streep.

Messina (Latin) Middle.

Mia (Italian) Mine. This charming name is extremely popular in America. *Miya*

Micah (Hebrew) Who is like God? A biblical name that's used for both genders.

Michaela (Hebrew) Who is like God? The feminine form of Michael. *Mckayla*, *Mikayla*, *Mikaela*

Michelle (French) Who is like God? Stylish, but fading in popularity.

Mila (Slavic) Loved by the people.

Milagros (Spanish) Miracles. *Mila*, *Milagritos*

Milan Name of the Italian city.

Milana (Slavic) Favoured. *Milania*

Mildred (English) Tender strength.

Milena (Czech) Grace.

Miley Famously created by the Cyrus family from the word smiley.

Milla (French) Church attendant. A short form of Camilla.

Millay Surname inspired by the poet Edna St. Vincent Millay.

Millicent (German) Industrious.

Millie (German) Industrious. Popular variation of Millicent.

Mina (German) Love. A character in *Dracula*.

Mindy (Latin) Honey; sweet. A short form of Melinda.

Minka (Polish) Strong-willed warrior.

Mira (Latin) Wondrous, admirable.

Mirabella, Mirabel (Latin) Wonderful.

Miracle (Latin) Wonder.

Miranda (Latin) Admirable.

Miriam, Maryam (Hebrew) Bitter.

Mirren Name of an Irish saint; meaning unknown.

Misty (English) Mist.

Moira (Irish) Bitter. Middle name of Wendy in J.M. Barrie's *Peter Pan*.

Molly (Irish) Bitter. *Mollie*

Mona (Irish) Noble.

Monday (English) Day of the week.

Monet Surname of the impressionist painter Claude Monet.

Monica (Latin) Advisor. *Monique*

Moray (Scottish) Great.

Montana Western United States place name.

Morgan (Irish) Circling sea of brightness.

Morven (English) A unisex name meaning large mountain and gap.

Moxie (English) Nerve; spirit.

Muna (Arabic) Desire.

Muriel (Irish) Bright as the sea.

Muse (Greek) Inspiration. Mythological word name and an English rock band.

Myla (American) Merciful. This name is newly in vogue as an alternative to Miley.

Myra (Latin) Fragrance.

We find delight in the beauty and happiness of children that makes the heart too big for the body.

RALPH WALDO EMERSON

Nadia (Russian) Hope. Brought to popularity by an Olympic gymnast. *Nadine*

Nahla (Arabic) Drink.

Nala (African) Successful. Heroine of *The Lion King*.

Nalani (Hawaiian) Serene skies.

Nancy (Hebrew) Grace.

Nanette (French) A combination of Ann and Nancy.

Naomi (Hebrew) Pleasant. A classic biblical classic that's enjoying a revival in popularity.

Natalie (Latin) Born on Christmas day. *Natalia*

Natasha (Greek) Born on Christmas day.

Navy A colour name also honouring a branch of the US military.

Nayeli (Native American)
I love you.

Neala (Irish) Champion.
Feminine form of Neal.

Neda (Slavic)
Born on Sunday.

Nell (English) Light.

Nelly, Nellie (English)
Light. A pioneer-era
abbreviation of Helen
and Eleanor.

Neola (Greek) Young girl.

Nerissa (Greek)
From the sea. Used in
Shakespeare's *The
Merchant of Venice*.

Nessa (Greek) Butterflies.
The short form of
Vanessa.

Nesta (Greek) Virginal,
chaste. Scottish form of
Agnes.

Netania (Hebrew) Gift
from God. Feminine form
of Nathan. *Netanya*

Netia (Hebrew) Plant.

Nevada (Spanish)
Covered in snow. The
name of a state in the US.

Nevaeh (American)
Heaven. Introduced in
2001, this trendy name
is 'heaven' spelled
backwards.

Neve (Latin) Snow.

Nia (Welsh) Bright.

Niamh (NEE-uv) (Irish)
Bright.

Nicole (French)
People of victory. *Nicki,
Nicolette, Nicola*

Nigella (Irish) Champion.
The elegant feminine form
of Nigel.

Nikita (Russian)
People of victory.

Nimesha (Hindu) Fast.

Nina (Spanish) Girl.
Ninette

Nisha (Hindu) Night.

Noelle (French)
Christmas. A charming
holiday name rising in
popularity.

Noemi (Spanish)
Pleasant.

Nola (Gaelic)
White shoulder.

Nona (Latin) Ninth.

Norah, Nora (Greek)
Light. Rising in the charts
since singer Norah Jones
appeared on the scene
in 2003.

Norma (Latin) Pattern.

Nova (Greek) New.

November The ninth
month.

Nuala (Irish)
White shoulders.

Nyla (Gaelic) Champion,
winner. *Nylah*

Nyree (Maori) Flaxen.

O

Oakley (English) Oak clearing. A nature name with a sharp-shooting namesake.

Oceana (Greek) Ocean.

Octavia (Latin) Eight.

October The eighth month.

Odele (Greek) Song.

Odessa (Greek) A long journey.

Odette (French) Wealthy. *Odile*

Oklahoma An American place name.

Oksana (Russian) Praise God.

Olga (Russian) Holy.

Oliana (Hawaiian) Oleander.

Olive (English) Olive tree. This name has vintage appeal.

Olivia (Latin) Olive tree. A top-ten name in the US.

Olwen (Welsh) White footprint.

Olympia (Greek) Mount Olympus. Home of the Greek gods and the Olympic games.

Ondrea (Scottish) Womanly. The Czech form of Andrea.

Onóra (Latin) Honour.

Opal (English) Gem.

Ophelia (Greek) Help.

Oralie (French) Golden.

Orchid The flower; a nature name.

Oriana (Latin) Sunrise.

Orillia A city in Ontario, Canada.

Orla (Irish) Golden princess. *Orlaith*

Orlanda (Italian) Famous land. The feminine form of Orlando.

Osana (Latin) Hosanna; Praise the Lord. *Osanna*

Ottilie (Czech) Wealthy. A feminine form of Otto. *Ottoline*

PQ

Padget, Paget (Greek)
Wisdom. *Padgett*

Padma (Hindu) The lotus.

Paige, Page (French)
Young helper, intern.

Paisley (Scottish) City in
Scotland also known for
the patterned fabric.

Paloma (Spanish) Dove. A stylish girl's name exemplified by Paloma Picasso.

Pamela (Greek) Honey. This name has a long history but has fallen in popularity. *Pam, Pamelina, Pammy*

Pandora (Greek) All-gifted. A name steeped in mythology.

Paola (Latin) Small. The feminine Spanish form of Paul.

Paris (English) A glamorous unisex name and the capital of France.

Parker (English) Park keeper. A unisex name that's currently more popular for boys.

Parvani (Hindu) Celebration. *Parvina*

Pascale (French) Child of Easter.

Patience A virtue name that was originally used more than a century ago.

Patricia (Latin) Noble. The feminine form of Patrick. *Pat, Patrice, Patty, Tricia, Trisha*

Paula (Latin) Small. *Pauleen, Paulina, Pavla, Polly*

Pavana (Hindu) Wind.

Pax (Latin) Peace.

Pearl (English) Pearl. A jewel name with Victorian spirit.

Peggy (English) Pearl. A variation of Margaret that was at its most popular from the 1920s to the 1950s.

Pela (Greek) Of the sea.

Pelagia (Greek) Of the sea. *Pela*

Pelika (Hawaiian) Peaceful.

Penelope (Greek) Weaver. Rooted in Greek mythology, with many charming variations. *Pela, Pen, Penny, Poppy*

Peony (English) Flower.

Pepper (English) Pepper plant.

Perla (Spanish) Pearl.

Persephone (Greek) Goddess of spring and rebirth. An epic mythology name.

Perry (English) Pear tree. A distinctive choice for a boy or a girl.

Petra, Petrova (Greek) Rock. Feminine form of the biblical name Peter. *Peta*

Petula An invented name created by the father of singer Petula Clark.

Peyton, Payton (English) Fighting man's estate. This unisex name is increasingly trendy.

Philippa (Greek) Lover of horses. Oddly, Philippa is more popular in England than the US. *Phil*, *Pippa*, *Pippie*, *Philippine*

Philomena (Greek) Lover of strength.

Phoebe (Greek) Brilliant, shining.

Phoenix (Greek) A mythical bird and the name of the capital of the US state of Arizona.

Phyllis, Phillida (Greek) Green leaves.

Picabo (Native American) Shining waters.

Piper (English) Flute player.

Pippa (English) Lover of horses. Diminutive of Phillipa and the name of the sister of the Duchess of Cambridge.

Pixie (English) Tiny.

Poet, Poetry A word name.

Polly (Hebrew) Bitter.

Pomona (Latin) Apple.

Poppy The flower.

Portia An ancient Roman tribal name used in Shakespeare's *The Merchant of Venice*.

Posy (English) Small flower bouquet.

Prairie Nature name.

Precious This name dropped in popularity after the 2009 release of the drama *Precious*.

Presley (English) Priest's meadow.

Primrose (English) First rose. One of the more accessible names used in *The Hunger Games*. *Prim*

Princess (English) Royal title.

Priscilla (English) Ancient. *Prissy*

Priya (Hindu) Beloved. The character in the sitcom *The Big Bang Theory*.

Promise Word name.

Prudence (Latin) Wariness. Quietly charming virtue name more popular in the UK.

Psalm (Hebrew) Song.

Purity (English) Pure.

Q

Queenie, Queen (English) Queen.

Quincy (English) The fifth son's estate.

Quinn (Irish) Advisor. This unisex name is just a little more popular for girls.

Quinta (Latin) The fifth.

Rachel, Rachael
(Hebrew) Lamb. An
ancient name that
became especially
popular in the 1990s.

Rae (Hebrew) Lamb.
A derivative of Rachel.

Raelyn, Raelynn (Hebrew) Lamb. A creative variation of Rae.

Rafaela (Hebrew) God has healed. Feminine form of Raphael. *Raphaela*

Rain, Raine A gentle-sounding nature name.

Raina, Reyna (Latin) Queen. A variation of Regina.

Rainbow A nature name that parents began to use occasionally in the 1970s.

Raleigh American place name with ties to the South.

Ramita (Sanskrit) Loved.

Ramona (Spanish) Protecting hands. Feminine form of Ramón. *Mona, Rimona*

Raquel (Spanish) Lamb. The Spanish form of Rachel.

Raven (English) The bird. Made more accessible by actress/singer Raven-Symone.

Raylene, Raylee (English) Lamb. Created from the name Rachel.

Rayna, Rayne (Hebrew) Song of the Lord. *Raina, Raine, Rana, Reyne*

Reagan (Irish) Son of the small ruler. *Raegan, Regan*

Rebecca, Rebekah (Hebrew) To tie or bind. This biblical name is an eternally popular timeless classic. *Becca, Becky, Reba, Rebeka, Riva*

Reese, Rhys (Welsh) Fiery, enthusiastic. The success of actress Reese Witherspoon made this a popular choice for girls.

Regina (Latin) Queen.

Reiko (Japanese) Pleasant child.

Reina (Spanish) Queen.

Reinette (Spanish) Queen. A variation of Reina.

Remy (French) Champagne. *Remi, Remie*

Rena (Hebrew) Melody; song of joy.

Renata (Latin) Reborn.

Renée (French) Reborn.

Rhea (Greek) Flowing river.

Rhiannon (Welsh) Goddess. *Rhiana, Rhianon, Riona*

Rhoda (Greek) Rose.

Rhonwen (Welsh) Slender, fair.

Ria (Spanish) River.

Rihanna (Arabic) Sweet basil. Now better known on account of the recording artist Rihanna.

Riley (Irish) Rye field.

Risa (French) Laughter.

Rishona (Hebrew) Initial; first.

Rita (English) Pearl. Made popular by Rita Hayworth in the 1940s.

River Nature name

Rivka (Hebrew) To tie or bind. Traditional form of Rebecca.

Roberta (English) Bright fame.

Robin (English) Bright fame; the bird. A variation of Robert and nature name.

Rochelle, Rachelle (French) Little rock.

Roma (Italian) Rome.

Romana (Italian) Rome.

Romilly (English) Spacious clearing. Surname and French place name with aristocratic connotations.

Rona (Scandinavian) Rough isle.

Rory (Irish) Red king.

Rosa, Rosie (Latin) Rose.

Rosalie, Rosalia French and Spanish forms of Rose.

Rosalind (German) Gentle horse. Used in Shakespeare's *As You Like It*. *Rosaleen, Rosaline, Rosalyn*

Rosamond (German) Famous protector. *Rosamund*

Rosanne (English) Rose; Grace. A combination of Rose and Anne. *Rosanne, Rosanna*

Rosario (Spanish) Rosary.

Rose (Latin) Flower. A pretty and popular choice for a middle name.

Rosemary (Latin) The rosemary plant. *Rosemarie*

Rosetta (Italian) Rose. A small Egyptian village where the Rosetta Stone was discovered.

Rowan (Gaelic) Red.

Rowena (German) Fame; joy.

Roxanne (Persian) Dawn. *Roxane, Roxie, Roxy*

Ruby (English) Jewel. Charmingly old-fashioned gem name that's recently increased in popularity.

Ruth (Hebrew) Friend. Classic biblical name that's due a comeback.

Ryan (Irish) Little king.

Rylan (English) Rye land.

Rylee (Irish) Rye field. Variant of Riley. *Ryleigh, Rylie*

S

Saanvi (Sanskrit) One who follows.

Sabella, Sabela (Spanish) God is my oath. Variation of Isabella.

Sabine (Latin) A Roman tribal name. *Sabina*

Sabrina A name from Celtic legend meaning river.

Sadhbh (syev) (Celtic) Sweet and lovely lady.

Sadie (Hebrew) Princess. Variation of Sarah with an old-fashioned feel.

Saffron (English) Flower, spice.

Sage (Latin) Wise.

Sahara (Arabic) Desert.

Sakari (Hindu) Sweet one.

Sakura (Japanese) Cherry.

Salem A Massachusetts place name.

Salina A Kansas place name.

Sally (Hebrew) Princess. Nickname for Sarah.

Salma (Arabic) Safe.

Salome (Hebrew) Peace.

Samantha (Hebrew) His name is God. An American combination of Samuel and Anthea. *Sam*, *Sammy*

Samara (Hebrew) Protected by God.

Samiya, Samiyah (Arabic) Understanding, forgiving.

Sana (Arabic) Shining.

Sandra (English) Man's defender. A diminutive of Alexandra.

Saniya, Saniyah (Hindi) Pearl.

Saoirse (SEER-sha) (Irish) Freedom

Sapphire (Hebrew) Jewel.

Sarah (Hebrew) Princess. Traditional biblical name. *Sadie*, *Salena*, *Sally*, *Sara*, *Sarai*, *Saretta*, *Sarita*

Sarala (Hindu) Straight.

Sariah, Sariyah (Hebrew) Princess.

Sasha (Russian) Man's defender. A variation of Alexander.

Saskia (Dutch) Meaning unknown. The name of Rembrandt's wife.

Savannah (Spanish) Open plains. This name was used in America as early as the 1880s.

Sawyer (English) Woodworker.

Scarlett (English) Red. Southern-belle image combined with a modern celebrity factor.

Scout An increasingly popular name that appears in *To Kill a Mockingbird*.

Seana (Irish) God is good. Feminine of Sean, an Irish variation of John.

Season (Latin) This name may bring spices to mind.

Sebastiane (Greek) Venerable, respected. Sebastian was an ancient Roman city.

Sedona A city in Arizona that could be used as a unique name.

Selah (Hebrew) A praise-laden exclamation and musical term that is used in the Bible.

Selena (Greek) Goddess of the moon. Made famous by singer Selena Quintanilla. *Celine*, *Selene*, *Selina*

Selima (Hebrew) Peace.

Selma (German) Helmet of God, safe.

Seona (SHO-na) (Scottish) God is gracious. Another form of Sean.

September (English) The month.

Sequoia A tribal name used for several places and a national park in California.

Seraphina (Hebrew) Angel. Chosen by Jennifer Garner and Ben Affleck for their daughter.

Serena (Latin) Serene. *Sarina*, *Serene*, *Serenna*

Serenity (Latin) This tranquil virtue name is gaining popularity in America.

Shaina (Hebrew) Beautiful.

Shakira (Arabic) Woman of grace. Colombian singer and dancer.

Shania Native American name meaning 'I'm on my way' made famous by singer Twain.

Shannon (Irish) Ancient. Popular in America in the 1970s and 1980s.

Sharon (Hebrew) A plain.

Shauna (English) God is good. A feminine form of John.

Shawn (Hebrew) God is good. Used more often for boys.

Shae (Hebrew) Request. *Shay*

Sheila (Gaelic) Blind. A colloquial term for girl or woman in Australia.

Shelby (English) Estate on a ledge.

Shelley (English) Meadow on a ledge.

Shenandoah Native American name meaning 'beautiful girl from the stars'.

Shiloh A biblical place name meaning 'he who is to be sent'.

Shira (Hebrew) Song.

Shirley (English) Bright meadow.

Shyla (Hindu) Daughter of the mountain. Name of the goddess Parvati.

Sibeta (Native American) Finding a fish under a rock.

Sibyl (Greek) Seer, oracle. *Cybill*, *Sibelle*, *Sybil*

Sicily Italian place name.

Sidra (Latin) Stars.

Sienna (Italian) Reddish-brown.

Sierra (Spanish) Mountain range.

Sigourney (English) Conqueror.

Silke (German) Blind. A variation of Cecilia.

Silvana (Italian) Woodland; forest.

Silvia (Latin) From the woods. *Sylvia*

Silvie (Latin) From the woods. A variation of Silvia. *Sylvie*

Simone (French) God listens.

Sinéad (shin-AID) (Irish) God's grace.

Siobhán (shuh-VAWN) (Irish) God's grace.

Sky, Skye (English) An ethereal word name; also an island in Scotland.

Skyler (Dutch) Shelter. A surname more commonly used for boys. *Skylar*

Sloane (Irish) Raider. *Sloan*

Snow (English) Word name that brings to mind a wintry scene.

Solange (French) Dignified, solemn.

Solara (Spanish) Sun.

Song An English word name.

Sonia (English) Wisdom. *Sonja, Sonya*

Sonnet A word name referring to a poem with 14 lines.

Sophia (Greek) Wisdom. *Sofia, Sophie*

Stacy (Greek) Resurrection. *Stacey*

Star A celestial word name. *Starla*

Stella (Latin) Star. A lovely name that is rising rapidly in popularity.

Stephanie (English) Crown.

Stormy A rarely used weather-related name. *Storm*

Story Word name with a tale to tell.

Sukey (English) Lily. An unusual but spirited form of Susan. *Suky*

Summer A seasonal word name that evokes warmth and abundance.

Sunday Day of the week originating with Old English for sun's day.

Sunshine A cheery word name that was most popular in 1975. *Sunny*

Suri (Hindu) Knife; (Persian) Rose. Famously chosen by Katie Holmes and Tom Cruise.

Susan (Hebrew) Lily. Shortened form of Susanna popular in the mid-1900s.

Susanna, Susannah (Hebrew) Lily. An ancient Hebrew name.

Suzu (Japanese) Bell.

Svetlana (Russian) Star.

Sydney (French) St. Denis; (English) Wide riverside meadow. *Sidney*

Sylvia (Latin) From the forest. *Silvia*

Sylvie (Latin) From the forest. *Sylvie*

Symphony Word name; an elaborate orchestral piece.

T

Tabitha (Aramaic) Gazelle.

Tahira (Arabic) Pure, chaste.

Talia (Hebrew) Dew.

Talitha (English) Girl.

Tallulah (Irish) Lady of abundance. Currently popular; chosen by Demi Moore and Bruce Willis for their daughter.

Tamara (Hebrew) Palm tree. *Tamia, Tammy*

Tamasine (Aramaic) Twin. An unusual feminine form of Thomas. *Tamsin*

Tamika (Japanese) Child of the people.

Tandy (English) Manly; brave. A feminine form of Andrew. *Thandie*

Tanith (Irish) Estate.

Tanya (Russian) Praiseworthy.

Tara (Irish) Hill. Used in *Gone with the Wind*.

Tarani (Hindu) Light.

Taryn (Irish) Hill. A newly created name stemming from Tara.

Tasha (Greek) Born on Christmas day.

Tatiana A Russian name that refers to an ancient Slavic king. *Tania, Tanya*

Tatum (English) Tate's homestead. Made feminine by actress Tatum O'Neal. *Taytum*

Tavora (Hebrew) From Mount Tavor.

Tawny (Irish) Golden brown. *Tawnee*

Taylor An English occupational name made famous by the singer-songwriter Taylor Swift. *Tailor*

Téa (Italian) Harvest. A charming and feminine variation of Teresa.

Teagan (Irish) Little poet. A fashionable US choice in recent years. *Tegan*

Temperance (Latin) Moderation. A little-known or used virtue name.

Tenley (English) Denis's field.

Teresa (Greek) Harvest. *Teri, Tess, Theresa*

Tertia (Latin) Third.

Tesla This surname has a steampunk edge, thanks to inventor Nikola Tesla.

Tess (Greek) Harvest. Short form of Teresa. *Tessa*

Thea (Greek) Goddess of light.

Thelma (Greek) Will.

Theodora (Greek) Gift of God.

Theta A Greek letter.

Tia (Spanish) Aunt.

Tiana (Spanish) Fairy queen. Used in Disney's *The Princess and the Frog*. *Tianna, Tiani*

Tiara (Spanish) Crown.

Tiffany (Greek) God's appearance. Fashionable 1980s name associated with prominent jeweller.

Tigris (Irish) Tiger.

Tilda (German) Maiden in battle. A shortened form of Matilda.

Timothea (Greek) Honouring God. The feminine form of Timothy.

Tina (Persian) Clay.

Tinley (English) Tyne's meadow.

Tinsley An Irish surname.

Tivona (Hebrew) Nature lover.

Toby (Hebrew) God is good. Form of Tobias that's more often used for boys.

Tomiko (Japanese) Content child.

Tori (Japanese) Bird. Also a nickname for Victoria.

Tracey (English) Summer. *Tracy*

Treasure (Latin) Highly valued.

Trilby A literary surname with English origins.

Trina (Greek) Pure. Variation of Katrina.

Trinity (Latin) Triad. Gained popularity after *The Matrix* was released.

Trisha (Latin) Noble. Variation of Patricia.

Trista (Latin) Sad.

Trixie (English) She brings happiness.

True A word name with honest overtones.

Trudy, Trudie (German) Spear of strength.

Tuesday Day of the week literally meaning day of Mars in Latin.

Twila (English) Double-woven.

Tyler (English) Maker of tiles.

Tyra (Scandinavian) Thor's battle.

Blessed be childhood, which brings down something of heaven into the midst of our rough earthliness.

HENRI FREDERIC AMIEL

girls

The stylish Irish

In the 1980s, Irish names reached far across the globe and influenced trends in America, Britain and other English-speaking countries. Today, the names parents are favouring may have been updated, but the Emerald Isle remains a top source of inspiration. Many of these names sound fresh even though they have historic roots.

Aisling	Enya	Morgan
Aislinn	Finley	Quinn
Ashlynn	Gemma	Reagan
Alana	Keira	Riley
Blaine	Kennedy	Saoirse
Cassidy	Kinley	Siobhán
Caylee	Maeve	Sloane
Ciara	Mairéad	Teagan
Darcy	Mckenzie	Una
Elaina	Molly	

Scottish stand-outs

Today's Scotland is more than the iconic kilts and bagpipes, and the girls' names are also full of surprises. Some are quintessentially Scottish, while others are less known. But all of these Scottish Gaelic names are contemporary choices with a distinctive, gentle sound.

Afton	Isla
Ailsa	Kenzie
Ainsley	Maisie
Cailyn	Ondrea
Caledonia	Paisley
Fergie	Skye
Fiona	
Ilsa	
Iona	

girls

Uma (Hindu) Flax.

Una (Irish) Lamb; (Latin) One. Used in *The Faerie Queene* by Edmund Spenser. *Euna*, *Yuna*

Unique When the other unique names just won't do.

Unity (English) Oneness.

Ursula (Latin) Little female bear.

Utopia State of perfection; invented by Sir Thomas More.

V

Valda (Norse) Ruler.

Valencia (Spanish) Brave, strong.

Valene An invented name probably created from the Spanish city of Valencia.

Valentina (Latin) Healthy. A romantic name that's slowly gaining favour with parents.

Valerie (Latin) Strong. *Valeria, Valorie*

Valletta A Mediterranean city, the capital of Malta.

Valora (Latin) Courageous.

Vanessa (Greek) Butterflies.

Vanora (Welsh) White wave.

Velma A name with English origins; meaning unknown.

Venus (Latin) The Roman goddess of love.

Vera (Slavic) Faith.

Verena (Latin) True.

Verity (Latin) Truth. A virtue name that still has some life left today.

Verna (Latin) Springtime.

Verona An Italian place name.

Veronica (Latin) True image.

Vespera (Latin) Evening star.

Vesta (Latin) Goddess of the home.

Vevina (Irish) Kind woman.

Victoria (Latin) Victory. A strong, classic name with royal connections. *Ria, Roria, Tori, Toria, Vicki, Vicky, Victoriana, Victorine, Victory*

Vida (Hebrew) Beloved.

Vienna A place name referring to the capital of Austria.

Viola (Scandinavian) Violet. One of the characters in Shakespeare's comedy *Twelfth Night*.

Violet (Latin) The colour; purple. Also a flower name. *Violetta*

Virginia (Latin) Virgin.

Vivian (Latin) Full of life. *Viviana, Vivienne*

Vivica (Latin) Full of life. *Vivicca, Viveka*

W X

Wanda (German) Wanderer.

Waverly (English) Meadow of quaking aspen.

Wendy Created by *Peter Pan* author J. M. Barrie.

Whitley (English) White meadow.

Whitney (English) White island.

Wilhelmina (German) Protector. A feminine form of William.

Willa (German) Protector. A short form of Wilhelmina.

Willow (English) The willow tree. A nature name.

Wilona (English) To desire.

Winifred (Welsh) Holy peace. Win, Winnie

Winona (Native American) Firstborn daughter. *Wynnona*

Winslow An English surname and place name referred to in the song 'Take it Easy'.

Winter The season. An evocative name with a pretty sound.

Wren The bird.

Wynne (Welsh) Fair, white. *Wynn*

Wyoming The state.

X

Xandra (Spanish) Protector. A form of Alexander.

Xanthe (Greek) Yellow.

Xaviera (English) New house. The feminine form of Xavier.

Xenia (Greek) Hospitable. *Xena*

Ximena (Spanish) Listening.

Xiomara (Greek) Guest, stranger.

Xylia (Greek) Forest.

Yadira (Hebrew) Friend.

Yael (Hebrew)
Mountain goat. *Yale*

Yamilet (Spanish)
Beautiful, elegant. *Yamileth*

Yareli A name of Spanish origin. Uncertain meaning.

Yaretzi (Aztec) You will always be loved.

Yaritza (Portuguese)
Small butterfly.

Yasmin (Persian)
Jasmine flower. *Yazmin*

Yesenia (Arabic) Flower.

Yoko (Japanese)
Child of the ocean.

Yolanda (Greek)
Purple flower. *Yolande*

Yoselin (Spanish) Member of the Germanic Gauts tribe.

Ysanne A created name combining Ysabel and Anne.

Yuliana A variation of Juliana, meaning youthful.

Yvette (French)
Arrow's bow.

Yvonne (French)
Yew wood.

z

Zaida (Arabic) Fortunate.

Zandra (English) Man's defender. A form of Sandra.

Zaniyah (Aztec) Forever; always.

Zanna (Hebrew) Lily. A variation of Susanna.

Zara (Hebrew) Dawn.

Zaria (Arabic) Rose. *Zariah*

Zaylee A created name derived from Bailey.

Zelda (German) Battle.

Zelia (Hebrew) Zealous, ardent.

Zelma (German)
Divine helmet.

Zena (Greek) Hospitable.

Zenobia (Greek)
Strength of Zeus.

Zephyrine (Greek)
Wind from the west.

Zia (Latin) Grain; (Italian) Aunt.

Zinnia (English) Flower.

Zippora (Hebrew) Little bird.

Zita (Greek) Seeker.

Ziva (Hebrew) Brilliant.

Zoe, Zoey (Greek) Life.

Zola (Latin) Earth.

Zsa Zsa (Hebrew) Lily. A variation of Susanna.

Zuleika (Arabic) Peace.

Zuri (African) Beautiful.

Zuzanna, Zuzu (Hebrew) Lily. A variation of Susanna.

Boys Names

Iker

Jayce

Robert

Theodore

Flynn

Amir

Brandon

Jacob

Paris

Alexander

Xavi

William

Max

Romeo

Maddox

Dante

A

Aarav (Sanskrit) Peaceful.

Aaron (Hebrew) Debated meaning. The name of Moses' brother in the Bible. *Aron*

Abbott (Hebrew) Father.

Abdiel (Hebrew) Servant of God.

Abdullah (Arabic) Servant of God.

Abel (Hebrew) Breath.

Aberdeen A city in Scotland.

Abijah (Hebrew) God is my father.

Abraham (Hebrew) Father of multitudes. A biblical patriarch. *Abe, Abram, Bram, Ibrahim*

Ace (English) Unity, one.

Adair (English) Spear of prosperity. A variation of Edgar.

Adam (Hebrew) Son of the red earth.

Adan (Spanish) Son of the red earth. A variation of Adam. *Aden*

Aditya (Sanskrit) The sun.

Adler (English) An eagle.

Adonis (Greek) Handsome. A name from Greek mythology.

Adrian (Latin) From Hadrian. *Adren, Adrien*

Adriel (Hebrew) God is my master.

Agustin (Latin) Majestic.

Ahmad (Arabic) More deserving.

Aiden (Irish) Little fiery one. A top-ten name in America. *Aaden, Aden, Aidan, Aidyn*

Akello (African) I have brought forth.

Alan (Celtic) Fair, handsome.

Alaric (German) Noble ruler.

Alban (Latin) White, blond.

Albert (English) Noble, bright. *Albie, Alberto*

Aldrich English surname meaning wise leader.

Alcott (English) Dweller at the old cottage.

Alden (English) Wise friend.

Alder (German) Alder tree.

Aldo (Italian) Wise, old.

Alec (Greek) Protector. A variation of Alexander.

Aled (Welsh) Child.

Alejandro (Greek) Protector. Spanish variation of Alexander.

Alexander (Greek) Protector. *Alex, Alessandro, Alessio, Alexzander, Alexis*

Alfie (English) Wise counsellor. A top-ten name in the UK.

Alfred (English) Wise counsellor. *Alfredo, Alfonso*

Alger (English) Clever warrior.

Ali (Arabic) Supreme, exalted.

Alijah (Hebrew) The Lord is my God. A spelling variation of Elijah.

Alistair (Greek) Protector. Variation of Alexander. *Alastair*

Allan (Celtic) Handsome. A spelling variant of Alan.

Alonzo (English) Wise counsellor. Spanish variation of Alfonso. *Alonso*

Altair (Greek) Bird.

Alvaro (German) All guard.

Alvin (German) Friend.

Amare (Sanskrit) Immortal.

Amari (Hebrew) Eternal.

Ambrose (Latin) Immortal one. The name of a saint and several literary characters.

Amir (Hebrew) Powerful.

Amory (German) Leader.

Amos (Hebrew) Strong one.

Anchor A distinctive oceanic word name.

Anderson (Greek) Son of Andrew.

Andrew (Greek) Manly. A much loved New Testament name. *Anders, Andres, Andre, Andy, Drew*

Andric Manly, a ruler. Derived from a surname.

Angel, Angelo (Italian, Spanish) Angel; messenger.

Angus (Scottish) Only choice.

Ansel (French) One who follows.

Anthony (Latin) Praiseworthy. *Antonio, Antoine*

Aodhan (Irish) Fire. Pronounced like Aiden.

Apollo (Greek)
Manly destroyer.

Aquilo (Greek) North wind.

Aram (Hebrew) Height.

Archer (English)
A bowman. A newly
fashionable name.
Arch, *Archie*

Archibald, Archie
(German) Bright, bold.

Ari, Ariel (Hebrew)
Lion of God.

Aries (Greek) The ram.

Aristotle (Greek) Superior.
Name of prominent ancient
Greek philosopher.

Arjun (Hindu) White.

Arlo (Spanish)
Bayberry tree.

Armand (German) Man
of the army. *Armando*

Armani (Persian) Desire.
Associated with fashion
designer Giorgio Armani.

Arnav (Sanskrit) Ocean.

Arnold (German) Strong
as an eagle. *Arnie*

Arrow A word name with
warrior appeal.

Arsenio (Greek) Virile.

Arthur (Celtic) Bear; rock.
Art, *Arturo*

Arvid (Scandinavian)
Eagle in a tree.

Asa (Hebrew) doctor.

Ashby (English)
Ash tree farm.

Asher (Hebrew) Happy.
One of Jacob's sons in
the Bible.

Ashley (English) Meadow
of ash trees. This name is
also popular for girls.

Ashton (English)
Town with ash trees.

Aspen (English) The tree.
A nature name and
Colorado place name.

Atticus (Latin) From
Athens. An increasingly
fashionable 'new/old'
name.

Auden (English) Old friend.

August, Augustus The
eighth month, and Latin
for great; venerable.

Aulay (Scottish) Forefather.

Austin (English) Majestic.
Texas place name.

Autry (French)
Ancient power.

Avery (English) Counsellor.

Aviv (Hebrew) Spring.

Axel (Scandinavian)
Father of peace.

Ayaan (Arabic) Lucky.

Azariah (Hebrew) God
helps. *Azarael*, *Azareel*

Azure (French) Blue.

Baden (German)
A bather.

Bainbridge (English)
Bridge over the river.

Baird (Irish)
An itinerant singer.

Balendin (Latin) Fierce.

Balin (Hindu) Soldier.

Banin (Irish) White.

Banner (English)
Flag bearer.

Banning (Irish)
Small, fair one.

Barack (Arabic) Blessing.
Now forever linked to
President Barack Obama.

Barclay (English) Valley
of the birches.

Barnabas (Hebrew)
Comfort. *Barnaby*, *Barney*

Baron (English) Warrior.

Barrett (English) Dispute.

Barry (Irish) Spear.

Bartholomew (English)
Farmer's son.

Bartram (English) Fame.

Basil (Greek) Regal.

Baxter (English) Baker.

Bay (Vietnamese) Born on Saturday; seventh child.

Baylor Surname and the name of several universities in Texas. *Bay*

Beacan (Irish) Small.

Beacher, Beach (English) Near beech trees.

Beau, Bo (French) Handsome.

Beauregard (French) Beautiful gaze.

Beck (English) Brook.

Beckett (English) Dweller near the brook.

Beckham (English) Home by a stream.

Bellamy (English) Handsome companion.

Benedict (English) Blessed. Name of actor Benedict Cumberbatch.

Benjamin (Hebrew) Son at my right hand. *Ben*

Bennett (English) Blessed. A variant of Benedict.

Benson (English) Son of Ben.

Bentley (English) Meadow. *Bentlee*

Benton (English) Town in Britain.

Benzi (Hebrew) Good son.

Berkeley (English) A surname and California college town.

Bernard (German) Brave.

Berry (English) Flower.

Bertie (English) Bright light.

Berwin (Welsh) White hair.

Bevan (Welsh) Son of Evan.

Bilal (Arabic) Chosen one.

Billy (English) Protector. Short form of William.

Bing (German) A hollow in the earth shaped like a kettle.

Birch (English) The tree.

Bishop (English) Bishop; a high-ranking clergy member.

Bix (English) A nickname for Bixby.

Bjorn (Scandinavian) Bear.

Blaine (Gaelic) Thin.

Blair (English) Flat piece of land. A more common choice for girls.

Blaise (French) Stutterer. Has attracted growing interest in recent years.

Blake (English) This name means both black and light.

Blaze (French) Stutterer. A fiery variation of Blaise.

Blue A color name popular among celebrities.

Boaz (Hebrew) Quick.

Bobby (English) Bright fame. A short form of Robert. *Bob*

Bodhi (Sanskrit) Awakening.

Bogart (French) Strength of a bow.

Bolt A lightning-fast word name, associated with Jamaican sprinter Usain.

Booker (English) Scribe.

Boone (French) Good; a blessing. Popularized by Daniel Boone.

Boris (Slavic) Warrior.

Boston (English) A city name.

Bowen (Gaelic) Small son.

Bowie (Gaelic) Blond.

Boyd (Scottish) Blond.

Bracken A unisex name and surname, also the name of a fern.

Braden (English) Broad meadow.

Bradley, Brad (English) Wide meadow.

Brady (English) Wide island.

Bram (Hebrew) Father of multitudes. A diminutive of Abraham.

Branch A nature name.

Brandon (English) Sword. *Branden*

Branson (English) Son of Brandon.

Brantley (English) Brand; fiery torch.

Braxton (English) Brock's town.

Brayan (Irish) Brave, virtuous. A spelling variation of Brian.

Brayden (English) From Brayden; broad valley. Popular in the US. *Braydon, Braeden, Braiden*

Braylon A name inspired by Brian and Brayden. *Bralin, Braylen*

Breccan (Irish) Freckled. *Brecken*

Breeze A nature name with an airy feel.

Brencis (Czech) Crown of laurel.

Brendan (Irish) Prince. *Brendon, Brenden*

Brennan (Irish) Descendant of sorrow. *Brennen*

Brent (English) Dweller by the burnt land.

Brenton (English) A variation of Brent and a surname.

Brett (Celtic) From Britain.

Brian (Irish) Brave, virtuous. *Bryan*

Brice (Celtic) Bright strength.

Brick (German) Swamp. Also an English word name.

Bridger (English) One who lives near a bridge.

Brigham (English) Village near a bridge. Name of Latter-day Saints' leader Brigham Young. *Brig*

Brighton (English) Bright town. Also a famed coastal town in England.

Brock (English) Badger.

Broderick (Scottish) Brother.

Brodney (Slavic) Person who dwells near a stream.

Brody (Scottish) Muddy place; ditch. *Brodie*

Brogan (Irish) Sturdy shoe.

Bromley (English) Broom hill. *Brom*

Bronson (English) Son of one with dark hair.

Bronze Exotic-sounding metallic word name.

Brooks (English) Brook, stream. *Brook*, *Brooke*

Broughton (English) Broken land.

Bruce (Scottish) From the brushwood thicket.

Bruno (German) Brown.

Bryant (Irish) Brave, virtuous.

Bryce An English given name and surname of unknown origin. *Bryson*

Brychan (Welsh) Speckled.

Bryn (Welsh) Hill.

Buck (English) A male deer. Also a surname. *Buckley*

Buddy (English) Friend.

Burgess (English) Citizen.

Burke (French) From the fortress. A strong and simple name choice.

Busby (Scottish) Village in a forest.

Byram (English) A cow barn. Variation of Byron.

Byron (English) At the cow barn. Also has a romantic literary connection because of its association with the poet Lord Byron.

boys

Cable (English)
Rope maker.

Cadby (English)
Soldier's estate.

C

Cade (English)
Round, barrel. *Kade*

Cadell (Welsh)
Small battle.

Caden Created from an
Irish surname and gaining
popularity in the US.
*Caiden, Cayden, Kayden,
Kaden*

Cael (Scottish) People of
victory. Scottish form of
Nicholas. *Caelan, Callan,
Callon, Calyn*

Caesar (Latin)
Long-haired. *César*

Cai (Welsh) Joy.

Cain (Hebrew) Spear.
Kane

Caius (Latin) Rejoice.

Calder (English)
Rocky water.

Cale (Irish) Slender. A
surname that may also
have links with Caleb.

Caleb (Hebrew)
Brave, bold. *Kaleb*

Calixte (Latin)
Most beautiful. *Calixto*

Callen (Scottish) Rock.
Callan

Calloway (Irish)
Rocky place. A surname
associated with both
golf and jazz. *Callum*

Calvin (Latin) Bald.
A sweet, simple name
with ties to John Calvin
and Calvin Klein.

Camden (English)
Twisting valley. Both a
surname and a place
name. *Camdyn, Kamden*

Cameron (Gaelic)
Crooked nose. *Camren,
Camron, Kameron*

Camilo (French)
Church attendant.

Campbell (Scottish)
Crooked mouth.

Cannon (English)
Clergyman. This name
has a tough edge
because of its warlike
associations.

Canyon An unusual and
intriguing nature name.

Caolan (Irish) Slender.

Cappi (Italian) Luck.

Captain (English)
In charge.

Carl (English) Man.
Variation of Charles.
Carlos

Carmelo (Hebrew, Italian)
Garden.

Carson (Irish) Son who
lives in a swamp. *Karson*

Carter (English)
Cart driver. *Cartier*

Carver (English) Sculptor.

Cary (English) Stream.

Case (English) He who
brings peace. *Casen,
Cason, Cayson, Kasen*

Casey (Irish) Brave in
battle.

Cash (Latin) Vain. Short
form of Cassius with
country swagger. *Kash*

Casimir (Polish)
He brings peace.

Casper (English)
Treasurer. Traditionally a biblical character as well as a friendly ghost.

Caspian A Persian name referring to the Caspian Sea. Also immortalized in the classic C. S. Lewis children's book *Prince Caspian*.

Cassian (Latin) Just, fair.

Cassiel (CASS-ee-el) (Latin) The angel of Capricorns in the Kabbalah tradition.

Cassius (Latin) Hollow.

Castle A word name as well as a surname.

Cathal (Irish)
Ready for war.

Cato (Latin) Smart.

Cavan (Irish)
Good looking.

Cedar A tree name with a sound that fits in with other Ce- names.

Cecil (Latin) Blind.

Cedric (Welsh)
Leader in war.

Cephas (Hebrew) Rock.

Cephas (Hebrew) Rock. An ancient, biblical name.

Chad (English) Protector.

Chaim (Hebrew) Life. Associated with the Jewish salutation *l'chaim*, meaning 'To life!' and used mainly during toasts.

Chance (English)
Good fortune.

Chandler (English)
Candle maker.

Channing (English)
Wise; church official.

Charles (English) Man. *Charlie*, *Chaz*, *Chip*, *Chuck*

Charlton (English)
House or town of Charles. *Carlton*

Chase (French) Hunter.

Chaucer (English)
Breeches maker. This name honours the father of English literature.

Chayton (Native American) Falcon.

Chen (Chinese) Great.

Chester (English)
Camp of soldiers.

Chip (English) Man. One of the many short forms of Charles.

Christian (English)
Anointed one; follower of Christ. *Crisitan*, *Cristiano*

Christopher (Greek) One who holds Christ in his heart. *Cristopher*, *Chris*

Cian (KEE-an) (Irish)
Ancient.

Ciaran (kee-AR-an) (Irish) Black.

Cillian (Irish) War. *Killian*

Cisco (Spanish) Frenchman. Short form of Francisco.

Clancy (Irish) Red-haired warrior.

Clarence (English) Clear.

Clark (English) Scholar.

Claud (Latin) With a limp. *Claude, Claudio*

Clay (English) Maker of clay.

Clayton (English) Clay settlement.

Clement (Latin) Merciful.

Clinton (English) Town near a hill.

Clive (English) Cliff.

Coby (Hebrew) Supplanter. A diminutive of Jacob. *Cobe, Kobe*

Cody (English) Cushion.

Cohen (Hebrew) Priest. A common Jewish surname borne by a few celebrities. *Coen*

Colby (English) Coal village. *Kolby*

Cole (English) Coal; dark. *Kole*

Coleman (Irish) Little dove.

Colin (Scottish) Young pup. *Collin*

Colt Word name recalling a young male horse and a type of firearm.

Colter (English) A herd of colts.

Colton (English) One from a dark town. *Colten, Kolton*

Colum (Latin) Dove.

Conlan (Irish) Hero.

Connor (Irish) Lover of hounds. A consistently popular name. *Conner, Conor*

Conrad (German) Courageous advisor.

Constantine (English) Stable, steadfast.

Cooper (English) Barrel maker.

Corbin (Latin) Raven. Associated with actors Corbin Bleu and Corbin Bernsen. *Corban, Korbin*

Cordovan (Spanish) From Cordova.

Corey (Irish) From the hollow. *Cory*

Coriander A spice name that sounds like a combination of Corey and Alexander.

Cormac (Gaelic) Raven.

Cornelius (Latin) Horn. Roman tribal name now usually reserved for novels.

Cort (German) Courageous.

Cortez (Spanish) Courteous. Surname of South American explorer.

Cortland Derived from an English surname meaning farmland.

Cosmo (Greek) Order. Kramer's surprising first name in the sitcom *Seinfeld*.

Costello A common Irish surname with a jaunty ring.

Cove An intriguing, beachy nature name.

Craig (Scottish) Rock.

Creed (Latin) Belief.

Creighton (English) Rocky area.

Creon (Greek) Prince.

Crew An unusual preppy-sounding word name.

Crispin (Latin) Curly hair.

Croix (croy) (French) Cross. St Croix is the largest of the American Virgin Islands.

Crosby (English) By the cross.

Cruz (Spanish) Cross. A stylish and common surname.

Cullen (Irish) Puppy, cub. Name used in the *Twilight* series of fantasy novels.

Curran (Irish) Hero.

Curtis (French) Polite.

Cyprian (Greek) Man from Cyprus.

Cyrus (Latin) Sun. Celebrity surname with a sunny disposition. *Cy*

Give a little love to a child, and you get a great deal back.

JOHN RUSKIN

D

Dabney (French) A person from one of several places in northern France called Aubigny.

Dagan (Hebrew) Grain.

Daithi (Irish) Swift, nimble.

Dakota (Native American) Friend. A place name that has been adopted as both a boys' and a girls' name.

Dale (English) One who lives in a valley.

Dallas A Scottish surname and place name in Scotland and Texas.

Dallin, Dallon (English) From the valley.

D

Dalton (English)
A town in the valley.

Damari (Spanish)
To tame. *Damarion*

Damian (Greek) Tame.
Becoming fashionable
thanks to the success of
the actor Damian Lewis.
Damien, Damion, Damon

Dane (English)
From Denmark.

Dangelo, D'Angelo
(Italian) From an angel.

Danger Austin Powers's
middle name.

Daniel (Hebrew) God is
my judge. A very popular,
classic biblical name.
Danny, Dan

Dante (Latin) Everlasting.
Great Italian poet's name.

Dara (Cambodian) Stars.

Darby (English) Area
where deer graze.

Darcy (Irish) Dark one.
Unisex name perfect for
a Jane Austen fan.

Darian (Greek) Wealthy.
A variation of Darius. *Darien*

Darius (Greek) Wealthy.

Dario (Latin) Wealthy.

Darnell (English)
Hiding place.

Darragh (Irish) Dark oak.
A unisex name. *Darrah*

Darrell (English) Dear one.
Darryl

Darren (Irish) Great.

Darshan (Hindu) To see.

Darwin (English) Friend.

Dashiell An attractive
Scottish surname;
meaning unknown. *Dash*

Davian An invented
name inspired by David.
Davion, Davon

David (Hebrew)
Cherished. An enduring
biblical classic. *Dave,
Davin, Davis, Dafydd*

Davin (Scandinavian)
Shining.

Davis (English)
Son of David.

Dawson An English
surname made famous
by the show *Dawson's
Creek*.

Dax A town in southwest
France. *Daxton*

Dayton (English)
Illuminated city.

Deacon (Greek)
Messenger, servant.

Dean (English) Valley.

DeAndre, D'Andre
A created name meaning
son of Andrew.

Decatur Commonly
chosen name for towns
inthe US to honour naval
officer Stephen Decatur.

Decker (German) Roofer.

Declan An Irish saint's
name with unknown
meaning.

Deegan (Irish)
Black-haired.

boys

91

Delacroix (French) Of the cross. This surname honours the French Romantic artist Eugène Delacrois.

Dell (English) Valley.

Delsin (Native American) He is so.

Demarco A created name that means of Mark. *Demarcus*

Demetrius (Greek) Lover of the earth.

Denali The name of a national park in Alaska.

Denby (Scandinavian) Denmark village.

Dennis (Greek) Follower of Dionysius.

Denver (English) Green valley.

Denzel (English) From the high stronghold. Star-powered but waning in popularity.

Deon (Greek) Follower of Dionysius.

Derby (English) Village with deer.

Derek (English) Leader. *Derick*, *Derrick*

Dermot (Irish) Free man. Actor Dermot Mulroney made this name more familiar.

Deshawn A created name meaning son of Shawn.

Desmond A surname and Irish place name.

Destry (French) War horse. Name used in the film *Destry Rides Again*.

Deverell (English) Riverbank.

Devon (Irish) Poet. An English place name. *Devin*, *Devan*

Dewey (Hebrew) Cherished. A variation of David.

Dexter (Latin) Right-handed. Gaining more exposure thanks to the TV drama of the same name.

Dickson (Scottish) Son of Dick. *Dixon*

Diego (Spanish) Supplanter. The Spanish form of James.

Dieter (German) People's army.

Digby (English) Village by a ditch.

Dillon (Irish) Loyal.

Dimitri (Russian) Lover of the earth. *Dimitr*, *Dimitrios*, *Dmitri*

Dino (Italian) A short form of names ending in -dino.

Dion (Greek) Follower of Dionysius. Heart-throb singer of the 1960s.

Dobbin (Scottish) Bright fame. A variation of Robert.

Dobry (Polish) Good.

Dolan (Irish) Black hair.

Dominic (English) Of the Lord. Traditionally used for boys born on Sunday. *Dom, Dominik, Dominique*

Donald (Scottish) Mighty.

Donato (Italian) Gift of God.

Donnelly (Irish) Dark-haired fighter. A common Irish surname.

Donovan (Irish) Dark.

Donte (Italian) Lasting.

Dorian (Greek) From Doris.

Dougal (Scottish) Dark stranger.

Douglas (English) Dark water.

Dov (Hebrew) Bear.

Dow (Irish) Dark hair.

Drake (English) Dragon.

Draven A surname that's used in the movie and comic book series *The Crow* by American artist James O'Barr.

Drew (Greek) Manly. A short form of Andrew.

Drystan (Welsh) Sad.

Dudley (English) Field where people gather.

Duncan (Scottish) Dark soldier.

Dunham (Celtic) Brown man.

Dunstan (English) Rocky hill.

Duriel (Hebrew) God is my home.

Dustin (English) Dusty place. Associated with the actor Dustin Hoffman. *Dusty*

Dutch Often used a nickname, most famously for Ronald Reagan.

Dwayne (Irish) Dark; Swarthy. *Duane*

Dwight (Flemish) Blond.

Dylan (Welsh) Son of the ocean. Has enjoyed a resurgence in popularity in recent years

Dyson A surname related to the name Dennis.

To have a name is to have a family, a legacy, and an identity.

ANONYMOUS

ε

Eachann (Irish) Horse keeper; horse lover.

Eallair (Scottish) Steward in a monastery. *Ellar*

Eamon (Irish) Rich protector.

Ean (Scottish) God is good. A variant spelling of Ian.

Earl (English)
An aristocratic title.

Easton (English) Eastern town. A surname and the given name of country singer Easton Corbin.

Eben (Hebrew) Stone. Related to the name Ebenezer.

Echo (Greek) A nymph from ancient mythology.

Eden (Hebrew) Paradise. This biblical place name is more often used for girls.

Edgar (English) Wealthy man who holds a spear.

Edison (English) Son of Edward. Inspired by inventor Thomas Edison.

Edmund (English) Wealthy guardian.

Edsel (English) Home of a wealthy man.

Edward (English) Wealthy guardian. Name with a noble history. *Edwin*, *Eduardo*, *Eddie*

Efrain (Hebrew) Fertile. The Spanish form of Ephraim.

Egan (Irish) Fire.

Eilam (Hebrew) For ever. Mentioned in the Bible. *Elam*

Eladio (Spanish) Man from Greece.

Elam (Hebrew) For ever. Variation of Eilam and an ancient civilization.

Elbert (English) Noble; shining.

Eledon (English) Leader's hill.

Elijah (Hebrew) The Lord is my God. Name of an Old Testament prophet. *Elian*, *Elias*, *Eliaz*, *Eli*

Elisha (Hebrew) God is my salvation. A distinctive biblical name. *Eliseo*

Ellard (German) Noble; brave.

Elliot (English) God on high. *Eliott*

Ellis (Hebrew) God is my salvation. An English variation of Elisha.

Elton (English) Ella's town.

Elric (English) Wise ruler.

Elvis (Scandinavian) Wise.

Elwyn (Welsh) Fair.

Emanuel (Hebrew) God is with us.

Emeril A French name of unknown meaning; popularized by the American chef Emeril Legasse.

Emerson (German) Emery's son. A unisex surname gaining favour as a name for girls.

Emery (German) Leader of the house.

Emile (Latin) Eager. *Aimil*, *Emilio*, *Emiliano*

boys

Emlyn (Welsh) Charming.

Emmett (Hebrew) Truthful. *Emmet, Emmitt*

Emrys (Welsh) Immortal. A variation of Ambrose.

Enapay (Native American) Courageous.

Enoch (Hebrew) Dedicated. From the Old Testament.

Enrique (Italian) Leader of the house. A variation of Henry.

Enzo (Italian) To win.

Eoghan (Scottish) Youth. A variation of Owen.

Eoin (Irish) God is good. A variant of Ian, which comes from John.

Ephraim (Hebrew) Fertile.

Eppa (Greek) Charming.

Erasmus (Greek) Loved.

Eric (Scandinavian) Ruler of the people. *Erick, Erik*

Erland (English) Land of a nobleman.

Ernest A virtue name originating from German. *Ernesto*

Errol The Scottish form of Earl, referring to the noble title.

Esket (Scandinavian) Divine cauldron.

Esmond (English) Rich protector.

Esteban (Spanish) Crown. The Spanish form of Stephen.

Ethan (Hebrew) Steady. *Ethen*

Euan (Scottish) Youth. *Ewan*

Eugene (Greek) Well born. *Gene, Gino*

Evak (Hindu) Equal.

Evan (Welsh) God is good.

Evander (Greek) Good man.

Ever A word name meaning always.

Everett (English) Wild boar.

Everly (English) Boar meadow.

Evron (Hebrew) Fertile. A variation of Ephraim.

Evzen (Czech) Well born.

Ewing (English) Friend of the law.

Ezekiel (Hebrew) Strength of God. *Ezequiel*

Ezell An American surname of unknown origin.

Ezra (Hebrew) Helper. A biblical name also borne by poet Ezra Pound.

Great one-syllable baby names for boys

Parents are particularly drawn to these short-and-sweet options for use as a middle name or a first name, particularly where a lengthy surname is involved. No matter what the reason, these quick and spirited names are perfect for your bouncing baby boy.

Beau *or*	Gray *or*	Max
Bo	Grey	Nash
Blake	Hank	Paul
Bryce	Jack	Rhett
Cade	James	Sean
Cash	Jett	Shaun
Chance	John *or*	Shawn *or*
Drake	Jon	Cian
Drew	Joel	Seth
Finn *or*	Kai	Troy
Fynn	Luke	Zack *or*
Flynn	Mark *or*	Zach
Grant	Marc	Zane

eXceptional boys names

Everywhere you look, names are springing up that have an 'x' in them. You'll find this trend particularly among baby boys in America and other English-speaking countries. These names have a distinct hard 'ks' sound in the name. Some parents are creating new spellings by replacing a 'cks' with an 'x', making Jackson into Jaxon; while others are filling their 'x' craving by looking to names that were traditionally spelled using this consonant. Here are a few appealing options that reflect the 'x' trend.

Alex	Knox
Alexander	Lennox
Axel	Lex
Baxter	Maddox
Braxton	Max
Dax	Maxim
Dexter	Maximus
Felix	Maxwell
Fox	Paxton
Hendrix	Phoenix
Huxley	Saxon
Jax	Xander
Jaxon	Xavier

boys

F

Fabian (Latin) One who grows beans.

Fable A word name meaning a story that illustrates a moral lesson.

Fabrice (French) Skilled craftsman; one who works with his hands.

Falcon English name referring to the bird of prey.

Falkner (English) A surname meaning falconer.

Fane (English) Happy.

Farhan (Arabic) Pleasant.

Faris (Arabic) Knight.

Farren (English) Adventurous.

Felim (Irish) Ever good.

Felipe (Spanish) Lover of horses.

Felix (Latin) Happy.

Fenris A wolf in Scandinavian mythology.

Ferdinand (German) Courageous traveller.

Fergus (Scottish) Best choice.

Fernando (German) Bold voyager.

Ferris (Irish) Rock. Forever linked with Ferris Bueller, the kid who skipped school.

Fielding (English)
In the field.

Fife (Scottish) From Fife, an area in Scotland.

Finbar (Irish) Blond hair.

Finch A surname and nature name referring to the bird. *Fynch*

Fingall (Scottish)
Fair-haired stranger.

Finley (Irish) Fair hero. *Finlay*

Finn (Irish) From Finland. *Fynn*

Finnegan (Irish) Fair.

Finnian (Irish) Fair.

Fintan (Irish) Fair. Name of an Irish saint.

Fionn (Irish) Fair.

Fiorello (Italian)
Little flower.

Fisher A surname and occupational name.

Fitzpatrick (Irish)
Son of a statesman.

Fitzwilliam (Irish)
Son of a soldier.

Flann (Irish) Red hair. *Flaine*, *Flannery*

Fletcher (English)
One who makes arrows.

Flint (English) Stream; a fire-starting quartz.

Flip A diminutive of Felipe, borne by late comedian Flip Wilson.

Florent (French) Flower.

Floyd (Welsh) Grey hair.

Flynn (Irish) Red-haired man's son.

Fonzie A variant of Alfonso, meaning wise counsellor.

Forbes (Scottish) Field.

Ford (English) Dweller at the river crossing.

Forrest (French)
Woodsman.

Fortune (French) Lucky.

Fox The animal, also an English surname.

Francis (Latin) From France; free man. *Franco, Francisco*

Frank (Latin) From France; free man. A popular variation of Francis. *Frankie*

Franklin (English)
Free landowner.

Fraser (French) Strawberry. *Frasier*, *Frazier*

Frederick (German)
Merciful leader. *Fred, Freddie*, *Ricky*

Freedom (English) Liberty.

Frisco (Latin) From France; free man. Short form of Francisco.

Fritz (German)
Merciful leader. Variation of Frederick.

Fuller (English)
One who shrinks cloth.

G

Gable (German)
God is bright. Surname
of the actor Clark.

Gabriel (Hebrew)
Man of God.

Gael (English)
Speaker of Gaelic.

Gaetano (Italian)
From Gaeta. *Guy*

Gage (French) Pledge.
Gaige, *Gauge*

Galaxy A starry nature
name.

Galileo (Italian)
From Galilee.

Galvin (Irish) Sparrow.

Gamble (Norse) Old.
Also a risky word name.

Gareth (Welsh) Gentle.

Garner (Latin)
To harvest grain.

Garnet A dark red
gemstone.

Garrett (Irish)
Brave with a spear.

Garrick (English) One
who rules with a spear.

Garrison (English) Fort.

Garth (Norse) Gardener.

Gary (English) Spear.

Gaston (French) Man
from Gascony in France.

Gatlin (English) Kinsman.
Surname associated
with the Gatlin Brothers,
country-music singers.

Gavin (Welsh)
White falcon. *Gavyn*

Gemini (Latin) Twins.

Gene (English) Well born.
Popular in the 1930s and
1940s.

Genero (Latin) Generic.

Gennaro (Italian)
January.

Gent (English)
Gentleman.

Gentry (English)
Aristocracy. Surname with
American southern style.

Geoffrey (French)
Pledge of peace.

George (Greek) Farmer.

Gerald (German)
Ruler with a spear.

Gerard (German) Brave
with a spear. *Gerardo*

Geraint (Welsh)
An old man.

Gerwyn (Welsh) Fair love.

German (English)
From Germany.

Gervais (French)
Skilled with a spear.

Gethin (Welsh)
Dark skinned.

Gevariah (Hebrew)
God's might.

Giancarlo (Italian)
A combination of John
and Charles.

Gianni (Greek) God is good.

Gibson (English)
Son of Gilbert.

Gideon (Hebrew) Feller
of trees. A biblical name
gaining popularity.

Gift A word name
wrapped up in a bow.

Gilbert (German)
Bright pledge.

Gilberto (German)
Bright pledge. Spanish
form of Gilbert.

Gilby (Irish) Blond boy.

Gilead (Hebrew) Hill of
testimony; camel's hump.

Giles (Greek) Young goat.

Gillespie (Irish)
Servant of the bishop.

Gino (Italian) Ever living.

Giovani (Italian) God is
good. A variation of John.
Giovanni, Gio, Vannie

Giuseppe (Italian)
God will increase.

Givon (Hebrew) Hill.

Glen (Irish) Narrow valley.

Golden A valuable colour
name.

Gomer (English)
Good fight.

Gordon (English)
Round hill.

Grady (Irish) Noble;
famous. Favoured in the
1800s and again today.

Graham (English)
Gray house. A surname
also well liked as a given
name.

Grant (Scottish) Great.

Gray, Grey The colour.
A popular middle name
for celebrity babies.

Grayson (English)
Son of a man with grey
hair. *Graysen, Greyson*

Greeley (English)
Grey meadow. A city with
cowboy style in Colorado.

Gregory (Greek)
Observer, watchman.

Griffin (Welsh)
Strong fighter. Also a
variant spelling of the
mythical gryphon.

Griffith (Welsh)
Powerful leader.

Grover (English)
Grove of trees.

Guillermo (Spanish)
A variation of William.

Gulliver (Irish) Glutton.
From the novel *Gulliver's
Travels*.

Gunnar, Gunner
(Scandinavian) Battle.

Gunther (Scandinavian)
Battle.

Gus (English) Great;
venerable. A short form
of Augustus.

Gustavo (Swedish)
Staff of the gods. *Gustav*

Guthrie (Scottish) Windy
place. *Guthre, Guthry*

Guy (French) Guide;
forest.

Gwilym The Welsh form
of William.

Hadrian (Latin)
From the Adriatic.

Hagen (Irish) Home ruler.

Hale (English) Healthy.

Halian (Native American)
Downy.

Halston (English)
Village near the meadow.

Hamish (Scottish)
Supplanter. A variation
of James.

Hamlet (English) Village.
The eponymous hero in
Shakespeare's tragedy.

Hamza (Arabic)
Powerful; lion.

Hank (English) Ruler of
the estate. A short form
of Henry.

Hans (German)
A variation of Johannes.

Hansel (German) Short
form of Johannes and
a well-known fairy-tale
character.

Harbour A word name;
haven for ships in a storm.

Hardy (German) Brave.

Harley (English) From
the hare's meadow.

Harold (English)
Army leader.

Harper (English) Harp
player. Made popular by
the author Harper Lee.

Harrison (English)
Harry's son.

Harry (English) Ruler of
the estate. An alternative
form of Henry.

Harvey (French)
Eager in battle.

Hassan (Arabic)
Handsome.

Haven (English)
Sanctuary; safe place.

H

Hawk Strong nature name referring to the bird of prey.

Hayden (English) Hill of heather. *Haiden*

Hayes (English) Hedges.

Hayward (English) Protector of hedged area.

Heath (English) Open field. Borne by late actor Heath Ledger.

Heathcliff (English) Cliff near an open field. Famous from Emily Brontë's novel *Wuthering Heights* and TV series *The Cosby Show*.

Hector (Greek) Holding fast.

Hendrix Surname associated with guitarist Jimi Hendrix.

Henry (English) Ruler of the estate. Dignified, royal and dashing. *Hal, Hank, Harry*

Herbert (German) Shining army. *Herb*

Herschel (Hebrew) Deer.

Hezekiah (Hebrew) God strengthens. Biblical name that's making a comeback.

Hidalgo (Spanish) Nobleman.

Hobbes (English) Bright fame. Used in the comic strip *Calvin & Hobbes*.

Holbrook (English) Brook near the hollow.

Holden (English) Hollow valley.

Hollis (English) Near the holly bushes.

Hooper (English) Hoop maker.

Horace (Latin) Timekeeper. An old Roman tribal name.

Horizon A word name for the line between the earth and sky.

Houston (English) Town on a hill.

Howard (English) Noble watchman. *Howie, Ward*

Huckabee An English surname meaning river's bend. *Huck*

Huckleberry Mark Twain character with southern style. *Huck*

Hudson (English) Son of Hugh. Name of a river in New York.

Hugh (English) Intelligent. Many noblemen have had this name.

Hugo (German) Intelligent. A distinctive variation of Hugh.

Humphrey (German) Peaceful warrior.

Hunter (English) Hunter. Becoming quite popular in the US.

Hutton (English) Town on the bluff.

Huxley (English) Hugh's meadow. *Huxlee*

Hyde (English) A measure of land.

Ian (Scottish) God is good. Quintessentially British.

Ibrahim The Arabic form of Abraham.

Idan (Hebrew) An era; long period of time.

Idris (Welsh) Impulsive.

Iestyn (Welsh) Moral.

Ieuan (Welsh) God is gracious. Welsh form of John.

Ignacius (English) Fervent, on fire. *Ignacio, Iggy*

Ike (English) A shortened form of Isaac.

Iker (Basque) Visitation.

Ilario (Italian) Cheerful. Rooted in the word hilarious.

Ilias (Greek) The Lord is my God.

Illinois (French) Man. American place name.

Imran (Arabic) Host.

Inek (Polish) Boar friend.

Indiana American place name famously used in the Indiana Jones movies.

Indigo A colour name meaning deep blue.

Inigo (Spanish) Fervent; on fire. A variant of Ignatius.

Ioan The Romanian form of Johann.

Ira (Hebrew) Observant.

Irvin (Scottish) Handsome.

Irving (Scottish) Green river. Name of the late composer Irving Berlin.

Isaac (Hebrew) Laughter. Old Testament name with modern sensibilities.

Isaiah (Hebrew) God is salvation. A major biblical prophet. *Isai, Isaias*

Ishaan (Hindu) Sun.

Ishmael (Hebrew) God will hear. *Ismael*

Israel (Hebrew) Struggle with God. Old Testament and place name. *Izrael, Izzy*

Ivan (Czech) God is good.

Ivar (Norse) Yew bow; archer.

Ives (English) Yew wood.

Ivo (German) Yew wood.

F

Jabari (Arabic)
To comfort.

Jabez (Hebrew)
Born in pain.

Jace (Hebrew) God
is my salvation. Also a
variation of Jason. *Jase*

Jack (English) God is
good. A popular variation
of John.

Jackson (English)
Son of Jack.

Jacob (Hebrew)
Supplanter. The top boys'
name in America. *Jake*

Jacoby A variation of
Jacob.

Jaden An American
name derived from Jade.
Jayden, Jadyn, Jaiden

Jadiel (Hebrew)
God has heard.

Jadrien A creative
combination of Jay and
Adrian.

Jaegar (German) Hunger.
Jaggar, Jagger

Jaime The Spanish form
of James.

Jair (Hebrew) Jailer.

Jairo (Spanish) Jailer.

Jakob (Hebrew)
Supplanter. *Jake*

Jamal (Arabic)
Handsome.

Jamar A creative form of
Jamal. *Jamari, Jamarion*

James (Hebrew)
Supplanter. A classic
biblical name. *Jameson,
Jamie, Jamison, Jim,
Seumas, Jacques, Diego*

Jamir An invented name
inspired by Jamal.

Japheth (Hebrew)
He increases.

Jared (Hebrew)
He descends.

Jarek (Czech) Spring.

Jaron (Hebrew) To shout.

Jarrett (English)
Brave with a spear.

Jarvis (German) Honourable.

Jasiah (Hebrew)
God supports. A variant
spelling of Josiah.

Jason (Hebrew)
God is my salvation.

Jasper The English form
of Gaspar, an ancient name
with ties to the Three Wise
Men. *Casper*

Javier (Spanish)
Homeowner.

Javion (Latin) Greece. *Javon*

Jaxon (English) Son of Jack.
A modern form of Jackson.
Jaxson, Jaxen, Jax

Jaxton (English)
Jack's town.

Jay (Latin) Blue jay.

Jayce A modern name
created from initials J.C.

Jaylen An invented name
with its roots in Jay. *Jalen*

Jazz A musical word name.

Jean (French) God is good.

boys

Jedi An unusual *Star Wars* name.

Jedidiah (Hebrew) Beloved of the Lord. *Jed*

Jefferson (English) Son of Jeffrey.

Jeffrey (German) Peace.

Jenkin (Flemish) Little John.

Jensen (Scandinavian) God is gracious. A common surname.

Jeremiah (Hebrew) The Lord uplifts. A well-liked biblical name.

Jeremy (English) The Lord uplifts. Variation of Jeremiah.

Jericho A biblical place name.

Jermaine (German) From Germany. *Germaine*

Jerome (Greek) Sacred name. A Roman Catholic priest and saint.

Jerry (German) Ruler with a spear. Short form of Gerald.

Jersey (Polish) Farmer. A New England place name. *Jerzy*

Jesse (Hebrew) Gift; God exists. *Jessie*

Jesus (Hebrew) The Lord is my salvation.

Jethro (Hebrew) Fame.

Jett (English) Aeroplane. High-flying name favoured by celebrities.

Jimmy (Hebrew) Supplanter. A short form of James.

Jiovanni (Italian) God is good.

Joah (Hebrew) Name of God; brother.

Joaquin (Spanish) God will judge. Spanish form of Joachim.

Joel (Hebrew) God is Lord.

Johan German variation of John. *Johann*

John (Hebrew) God is good. *Jack, Jon, Jovi, Jovanni*

John-Paul Often used in honour of Pope John Paul II. *Johnpaul*

Jonah (Hebrew) Dove.

Jonas (Greek) Dove. Variation of Jonah.

Jonathan (Hebrew) Gift from God. A classic biblical name.

Jordan (Hebrew) To flow down. The river Jordan is where Jesus was baptized.

Jorge (Spanish) Farmer. Variation of George.

José (Spanish) God will increase. A very popular form of Joseph.

Joseph (Hebrew) God will increase. *Joe*, *Joey*

Joshua (Hebrew) God is my salvation. *Josh*, *Josue*

Josiah (Hebrew) God supports.

Joss (English) Merry one.

Journey A word name that's more often used for girls.

Juan (Spanish) God is good.

Judah (Hebrew) Praise. A sweet and strong Old Testament name.

Jude (Latin) Praise. A variation of Judah made popular in recent years by actor Jude Law.

Juke American slang meaning a suggestive dance.

Julian (Latin) Young.

Julio The Spanish form of Julius.

Julius (Latin) Young.

Jun (Chinese) Truth.

Junior (English) Young.

Juniper Unisex nature name used more often for girls.

Jupiter (Latin) Father. Planet name and the supreme god in Roman mythology.

Justice One of the few virtue names with masculine appeal. *Justus*

Justin (Latin) Just. *Justen*, *Justino*, *Justyn*

K...

Kade (English) Round.

Kaden A trendy variation of Kade.

Kadmiel (Hebrew) God is first.

Kael (Scottish) People of victory.

Kahanu (Hawaiian)
He breathes.

Kahil (Turkish) Young. *Kahlil*

Kai (Hawaiian) Sea.
This name is a rising star.

Kaj (Greek) Earth.

Kale (Hawaiian) Man.

Kaleb (Hebrew) Brave,
bold.

Kaleo (Hawaiian)
One voice.

Kamari A village on the
island of Santorini, Greece.

Kameron (Gaelic)
Crooked nose. A varied
spelling of Cameron.

Kangi (Native American)
Raven.

Kanye An African place
name now associated
with rapper Kanye West.

Kareem (Arabic)
Generous.

Karl (German) Man. *Karlen*

Karson (Irish) Son who
lives in a swamp.

Kasper (English)
Treasurer. A variation of
the historic name Casper.
Kaspar, Kacper

Kayden (English) Round.
A variation of Kade.
Kaden

Kayson A newly created
name that means son
of Cade.

Keanu (Hawaiian) Cool
mountain breeze. Known
for actor Keanu Reeves.

Keaton (English)
Hawk nest.

Keegan (Irish) Small and
passionate. *Keagan*

Keenan (Irish) Small,
ancient.

Keir (Irish) Swarthy.

Keiran A variation of Keir.

Keith (Scottish) Forest.

Kellen (Irish) Slender.
Kellan

Kelly (Irish) Warrior. Originally
a boy's name that has grown
more popular for girls.

Kelvin (Gaelic)
From the narrow river.

Kendal (English) Valley of
the river Kent in Cumbria.

Kendrick (English)
Royal hero.

Kenneth (Irish) Handsome.
Ken, Kenny

Kent (English) County in
England.

Kentucky A place name
referring to the bluegrass
state.

Kenway (English)
Brave fighter.

Kenyon (Irish) Blond.

Keon (Irish) Well born.

Keoni (Hawaiian)
God is good.

Kerr (Scandinavian) Swamp.

Kerry (Irish) County in
Ireland.

Kersen (Indonesian) Cherry.

Kevin (Irish) Handsome.

Keyon (English) Guide, leading.

Kian (Irish) Ancient. A variation of Cian.

Kiefer (German) Barrel maker.

Kieran (Irish) Dark.

Killian (Irish) Conflict.

Kincaid (Celtic) Leader in war.

King (English) King.

Kingsley (English) Meadow of the king.

Kingston (English) Town of the king. Name of a place near London.

Kipp (English) Hill with a peak.

Kirby (English) Settlement by a church.

Kirk (Norse) Church.

Knight A royal title associated with a medieval warrior.

Knox (English) Hills.

Kobe (Hebrew) Supplanter. A respelling of Cobe.

Kody (English) Cushion. A variation of Cody.

Kohen (Hebrew) Priest. From the name Cohen.

Kolton (English) One from a dark town. A variant spelling of Colton. *Kolten*

Konnor (Irish) Lover of hounds. A new variation of Connor.

Korbin (Latin) Raven. Corbin with a K.

Krish (Sanskrit) Dark.

Kristian The Greek form of Christian.

Kristopher A Greek variation of Christopher.

Kurt The German form of Kurtis.

Kyan A newly created variation of Ryan.

Kylan A modern name created from Kyle.

Kyle (Scottish) Narrow land.

Kyler (Gaelic) Church.

Kymani (African) Adventurous traveller. Ky-mani is the name of Bob Marley's son.

Kyo (Japanese) Cooperation or apricot.

Kyron A created name with roots in Tyrone and Kyle. *Kyran*

Kyros (Greek) Master.

Kyson A created name inspired by Tyson.

The fastest-rising boys' names in England and Wales

These trendy names have recently enjoyed an increase in popularity. They may not be as tried and tested as some of the classic names, but they are fashionable and just as well liked. These fast-risers from England and Wales tell us that parents there are particularly infatuated with boys' names that end in 'son' and sound like a surname, feel a little old-fashioned, or end in a vowel such as 'ie' or 'y'.

1 Tommy
2 Jenson
3 Jackson
4 Elijah
5 Blake
6 Frankie
7 Dexter
8 Arthur
9 Riley
10 Mason
11 Sebastian
12 Leo
13 Muhammad
14 Stanley
15 Bobby
16 Henry
17 Luca
18 Kayde
19 Aiden
20 Harrison
21 Jacob
22 Taylor
23 Isaac
24 Freddie
25 Edward

The fastest-rising boys' names in the US

These of-the-moment names have recently jumped in popularity. Parents may have discovered them through anything from a character in a novel to a political or sports figure. The hottest names for boys in America include an 'en', 'an' or 'on' suffix. Occupational names ending in 'er', such as Archer or Parker, are also hitting a sweet spot, as well as names that begin with an A.

1 Brantley
2 Iker
3 Maximiliano
4 Zaiden
5 Kamden
6 Barrett
7 Archer
8 Declan
9 Atticus
10 Nico
11 Abram
12 Amare
13 Maverick
14 Jayce
15 Dexter
16 Jameson
17 Remington
18 Kieran
19 Kason
20 Finnegan
21 Adriel
22 Bruce
23 Milo
24 Abel
25 Chandler

boys

L

Lachlan (Scottish) Hostile.

Lake A serene nature name.

Lamar (Latin) The sea.

Lamarcus Originating from the name Marcus, meaning warlike.

Lamont (Scandinavian) Man of law.

Lance (French) Servant. From the name Lancelot.

Landon (English) Grassy meadow.

Landry (French) Ruler. Surname of an American football player and coach.

Lane (English) A small path.

Larry (English) From Laurentium. A short form of Lawrence.

Lars (Scandinavian) From Laurentium.

Lathan (Scandinavian) The barn.

Lawrence (Latin) From Laurentium. *Laurence*

Lawson (English) Son of Laurence.

Layne A variation of Lane.

Lazarus (Hebrew) God's help. *Lazaro*

Leaf A nature name sometimes linked to the name Leif.

Leander (Greek)
Lion man. *Leandro*

Lee (English)
Pasture, meadow.

Legend A mythical word name.

Leif (Scandinavian)
Heir, descendant.

Leighton (English)
Meadow settlement.
Layton

Leland (English)
Meadow land.

Lennon (Irish) Small cape. Honours the late musician and songwriter John Lennon.

Lennox (Scottish)
Many elm trees.

Leonard (German)
Bold as a lion. *Leonardo*, *Leo*, *Leon*, *Leonidas*

Leopold (German)
Brave people.

Lester (English)
From Leicester.

Levi (Hebrew) Attached. Biblical name that also wears blue jeans.

Lewis An English surname meaning famous warrior.

Liam (German) Constant protector. A form of William that's particularly popular in Ireland.

Lincoln (English) Town by a pool. A presidential surname. *Linc*

Linden (English)
The linden tree.

Link A short form of Lincoln.

Linus (Greek) Flax.

Lionel (Latin) Little lion. *Leonel*

Llewellyn (Welsh)
Lionlike.

Lloyd (Welsh) Grey.

Logan (Irish) Hollow in a meadow.

London An English place name that's becoming more popular in the US.

Lorcan (Irish) Little fierce one.

Lorenzo The Italian form of Lawrence.

Louis (French) Famous warrior. Kingly name with a little jazz thrown in. *Luis*

Lucas (Latin) Man from Lucanus. A top name in the US. *Lukas*

Lucian (Latin) Light. *Luciano*

Luke (Greek) From Lucanus. Biblical gospel writer. *Luca*, *Luka*

Luther (German)
Army people.

Lyle (French) The island.

Lyric A musical word name used for both genders.

Lysander (Greek)
Liberator.

M

Macaulay (Scottish)
Son of the moral one.

Mack A short form
of names beginning
with Mac.

Madden A surname
famous in the US for its
association with shoe
designer Steve Madden.

Maddox (Welsh)
Fortunate. A variation
of Madoc.

Madoc (Welsh)
Fortunate.

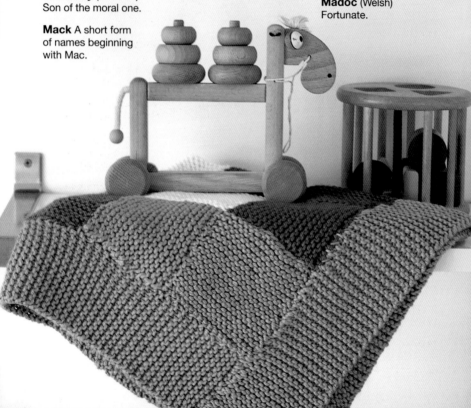

Madrid A place name; the capital of Spain.

Magnus (Latin) Great.

Mahir (Arabic) Capable.

Mahon (Irish) Bear.

Major (Latin) Greater.

Makai (American) Who is like God? A form of Michael.

Makhi (Greek) Battle.

Maksim (Roman) The greatest.

Malachi (Hebrew) Messenger. *Malachy*

Malcolm (English) A servant of St Columba.

Malik (Arabic) Master, king.

Mandel (German) Almond.

Mannix (Irish) Little monk.

Manuel (Spanish) God with us. More common than Emmanuel.

Marcus (Latin) Warlike. *Marc, Marco, Marcos*

Marcel (Latin) Young warrior. *Marcelo*

Mariano An Italian and Spanish form of Mars.

Mario (Italian) Roman tribal name.

Marius A Latin name probably originating from Mars, the god of war.

Mark (English) Warlike. Well-liked name that was at its most popular in the 1960s.

Marlon (French) Little hawk.

Marquis An English nobleman.

Marshall (French) One who cares for horses.

Martin (Latin) Warlike. *Mart, Marty*

Marvel A wonder. Word name with comic-book association.

Marvin (Welsh) Sea friend.

Mason (French) Stone carver.

Mather (English) Mighty army.

Matthew (Hebrew) Gift of the Lord. Name of a disciple of Jesus. *Mathias, Matias, Matteo*

Maurice (Latin) Dark skinned. *Maruicio*

Maverick (American) Nonconformist. Slowly rising in popularity.

Max A short form of names beginning with Max. *Maxx*

Maximilian (Latin) Greatest. *Maximiliano, Maximo*

Maximus, Maxim (Latin) Greatest.

Maxton (Latin) Great town.

Maxwell (Scottish) Marcus's stream.

Mayes The month of May.

Mekhi A variation of Malachi.

Melbourne A city in Australia.

Melvin (Irish) Great chief.

Memphis A unisex place name in Tennessee and ancient Egypt.

Mercer (French) Shopkeeper. *Merce*

Merrick (English) Dark skinned.

Merritt (English) Small and famous.

Messiah (Hebrew) Anointed one.

Micah (Hebrew) Who is like God? Appealing biblical name.

Michael (Hebrew) Who is like God? *Mike*, *Miguel*

Michelangelo An artist's name combining Michael and Angelo.

Michigan (French) Large lake. American place name.

Midnight The transition between two days.

Milagro (Spanish) Miracle.

Miles (Latin) Soldier. *Myles*

Miller (English) One who mills grain.

Milo (German) Generous.

Milton (English) Mill town.

Misael (Hebrew) Who is like God?

Mitchell A surname with roots in the name Michael.

Mitt A short form of Milton, which means mill town.

Mojave Native American place name.

Monaco A city state on the French Riviera.

Monroe (Irish) Red marsh.

Montana A western city and unisex place name used more often for girls.

Montel A created name of unknown meaning.

Monty A short form of Montague.

Mordecai (Hebrew) Warrior. Often used for boys born during Purim.

Morgan (Irish) Circling sea of brightness.

Moroccan From Morocco. Chosen by singer Mariah Carey and actor Nick Cannon for their son.

Morris (French) The moors.

boys

Mortimer (French)
Still water.

Morton (English)
Town by a moor.

Moses (Egyptian) Arrived by water. Hebrew leader and prophet. *Moises*

Moshe The Hebrew form of Moses.

Moss (English) Arrived by water. A nature name with connections to Moses.

Mostyn (Welsh)
Mossy settlement.

Muhammad (Arabic)
Praiseworthy. The founder of the Muslim faith. *Mohammed*

Murad (Arabic)
A wish fulfilled.

Murdo (Scottish) Sailor. Short form of Murdoch.

Murphy (Irish)
Sea fighter.

Murray (Scottish)
Mariner.

Musa (African) Child.

Mustafa (Arabic)
Chosen.

Myers (English)
One who lives in a swamp.

Myron (Greek)
Aromatic oil.

Every baby born into the world is a finer one than the last.

CHARLES DICKENS

Nabil (Arabic) Noble.

Nadir (Hebrew)
Precious; scarce.

Namaka (Hawaiian)
Eyes. The name of a
Hawaiian goddess.

Napoleon (Greek)
Lion of a new city.

Nash (English)
At the ash tree.

Nasir (Arabic) Helper.

Nathan (Hebrew)
Gift from God. An
attractive biblical name
with many variations.
*Nat, Nate, Nathaniel,
Nathanael, Natty, Thaniel*

Ned A shortened version
of Edward, meaning
wealthy guardian.

Nehemiah (Hebrew)
The Lord's comfort.

Neil (Irish) Champion.
Neal, Neill

Nelson (English)
Son of Neil.

Neo (Latin) New.

Neptune (Latin)
Roman god of the sea.

Nestor (Greek) Traveller.

Nevin (Irish) Holy.

Neville (French)
New town.

Newell (English)
New hall.

Niall (Irish) Champion.

Nicholas (Greek) People
of victory. *Nick, Nickolas,
Nico, Niko, Nikolai*

Nigel (Irish) Champion.
A form of Neil popular in
the UK during the 1950s
and 1960s.

Night A word name
associated with Indian-
American movie director
M. Night Shyamalan.

Ninian (Scottish)
Unknown meaning.

Nixon (English)
Son of Nicholas.

Noah (Hebrew) Rest.
Adorable and biblical.

Noble (Latin) Well bred.

Noe (Polish) Quiet.

Noel (French) Christmas.
A perfect holiday name.

Nolan (Irish)
Champion; noble.

Norman (English)
Northerner.

North An unusual,
elegant word name with
a strong direction.

Nuri (Arabic) Light.

Nye (Welsh) Honour.

*Every child begins
the world again.*

HENRY DAVID
THOREAU

boys

Oak, Oakley (English)
Tree; meadow of oak
trees.

Obadiah (Hebrew)
Servant of God.

Oberon (German)
Noble and bearlike.
Shakespearean name.
Auberon

Ocean A nature name
and surname from the
movie *Ocean's Eleven*.

Octavius (Latin)
Eighth child.

Odhrán (O-ran) (Irish)
Pale green.

Odin (Scandinavian)
A Norse god.

Oisín (Osh-een) (Irish)
Young deer. *Ossian*

Olaf (Scandinavian)
An heir, descendant.

Olery (French) Leader.

Olin (Scandinavian)
An heir, descendant.

Oliver (Latin) Olive tree.
A charming name
increasing in popularity.

Omar (Hebrew) Eloquent.

Omari (Hebrew)
Servant of God.

Ontario A Canadian
province.

Onyx A gemstone name
with a unique look and
sound.

Oran (Irish) Green.

Oren (Hebrew) Ash tree.

Oriel (Latin) Golden.

Orion (Greek) Hunter.
Mythology and
constellation name.

Orlando (Italian)
Famous land. Italian form
of Roland; borne by actor
Orlando Bloom.

Orson (Latin) Bearlike.

Orville (French)
Golden town.

Osbaldo (German)
God's power.

Oscar (English)
Divine spear.

Osian, Ossian
A legendary Welsh poet.

Osric (English)
Divine ruler.

Osvaldo (English)
Divine power. Spanish
form of Oswald.

Otis (English)
Son of Otto.

Otto (German) Wealthy.

Owen (Welsh) Well born.
Owain, Iwan

Oxford (English)
River crossing for oxen.

Oz (Hebrew) Power.
The magical land from
L. Frank Baum's novels.

Pablo (Spanish) Small. A popular variation of Paul.

Pacey A name based on the character Pacey Witter in *Dawson's Creek*. *Pace, Pacen, Payse*

Paco (Spanish) From France; free man.

Pádraic (Irish) Noble man. Variation of Patrick used in Ireland. *Pádraig*

Pagiel (Hebrew) Worships God; God allots.

Palmer (English) One who carries palm branches.

Paris A unisex place name referring to the legendary Trojan hero and the City of Light.

Parker (English)
Park keeper.

Parry (Welsh)
Son of Harry.

Pascal (English) Easter.
Surname of the great
thinker Blaise Pascal.

Patch A nickname often
derived from Peter.

Patrick (Irish) Noble man.
Charming Irish name
honouring St Patrick.

Paul (Latin) Small. An
ancient name with biblical
roots. *Pablo, Paolo,
Pashka, Povel, Pavlo*

Pax (Latin) Peace.

Paxton (English)
Peaceful town.

Paz (Hebrew) Golden.
(Spanish) Peace.

Pedro (Spanish) Rock.
A variation of Peter.

Peeta (Scandinavian)
Rock. Form of Peter used
in *The Hunger Games*.

Pelagios (Greek)
From the sea.

Pelham (English)
Peola's home.

Pembroke (Irish) Cliff.

Penley (English)
Fenced meadow.

Percy (French)
From Percy.

Peregrine (Latin)
Traveller. The appropriate
name of a falcon. *Perry*

Peter (Greek) Rock.
A cherished biblical name.

Peyton (English)
Soldier's estate. *Payton*

Philemon (Greek) Kiss.

Philip (Greek) Lover
of horses. *Phil, Phillip,
Phillipe, Filip, Pip*

Phoenix (Greek) Bright
red. A mythical bird and
the capital of Arizona.

Piaras (Greek) Rock.
A Gaelic form of Piers.

Pierce (Greek) Rock.
Piercy, Piers, Pearce

Pierre (French) Rock.
A variation of Peter.

Pollux (Greek) Crown.

Porter (Latin)
Gatekeeper.

Prentice (English)
Apprentice.

Prescott (English)
Priest's cottage.

Preston (English)
Priest's town.

Price (Welsh) Son of
an ardent man. *Pryce*

Prince (Latin)
The noble title.

Princeton (English)
Princely town.

Prosper (Latin)
Fortunate.

Pryderi (Welsh) Concern.

Putnam (English) One
who lives near a pond.

Q

Quade (Latin)
Born fourth.

Quarry A nature name.

Quentin (Latin) Fifth.
Quinten, Quintin, Quinton

Quest (Latin)
An arduous search.

Quigley (Irish)
One with messy hair.

Quillan (KIL-an) (Irish)
Cub.

Quimby (Norse)
A woman's estate.

Quincy (French)
Estate of the fifth son.

Quinlan (Irish)
Strong man.

Quinn (Irish) Wise.
A unisex name becoming
more popular for girls.

Quinto (Spanish)
Home ruler.

Racer A speedy
word name.

Radley (English)
Red meadow.

Raiden (Japanese)
God of thunder.

Raimi (Arabic) Fond.

Rainer (German)
Wise army. Borne
by German poet
Rainer Maria Rilke.
Raine

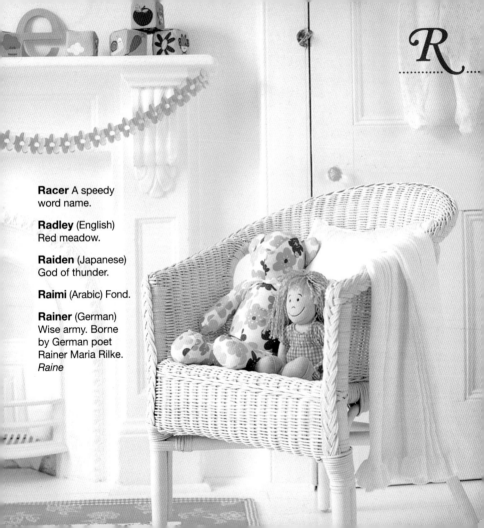

Raleigh (English) Deer meadow. A city in North Carolina.

Ralph (English) Wolf-counsellor. *Ralf*

Ramiro (Portuguese) Great judge.

Ramon The Spanish variation of Raymond.

Ramsay (English) Island of rams.

Randall (English) Wolf, shield. *Randy*

Randolph (English) Wolf, shield. *Ranoulf*

Ranger (French) Guardian of the forest.

Ransom (English) Shield's son.

Raphael (Hebrew) God has healed. Has spiritual and artistic qualities. *Rafael*

Rashad (Arabic) Moral work.

Rasmus (Greek) Beloved.

Raul The Spanish form of Ralph.

Ray (English) Wise.

Rayden A name from Japanese mythology.

Raylan Created from Ray, and linked to the US TV series *Justified*.

Raymond (German) Wise protector.

Reading (English) Son of a red-haired one.

Reagan (Irish) Little king.

Redmond (Irish) Counsellor.

Reece (Welsh) Fiery, zealous. *Reese*

Reginald (English) Strong counsellor. *Reggie*

Rehan (Armenian) Sweet basil.

Reid (English) Red-haired. *Reed*

Remington (English) A raven town. Has a steely, masculine feel. *Remy*

Rene (French) Reborn.

Reuben (Hebrew) Behold, a son. A biblical name and a corned-beef sandwich. *Ruben*

Rex (Latin) King.

Rey (Spanish) King.

Rhett (Welsh) Counsel, advice. Associated with Rhett Butler in *Gone with the Wind*.

Rhodes (Greek) Where roses grow.

Rhodri (Welsh) Wheel, ruler.

Rhys (Welsh) Ardour, enthusiasm.

Richard (German) Strong ruler. *Ricardo*, *Ricky*, *Rich*

Rigby (English)
Ridge farm.

Riley (Irish) Brave. *Rylee*

Ringo (Japanese) Apple.

Rio (Spanish) River.

Riordan (Irish)
Minstrel, poet.

Ripley (English)
A clearing; meadow.

River A nature name.

Roark (Irish) Mighty.

Robert (English)
Bright fame. Well liked
for centuries. *Bob*, *Bobby*,
Rob, *Robbie*, *Roberto*,
Rupert

Robin A variation of
Robert now considered
to be unisex.

Rocco (German) Rest.
Chosen by the singer
Madonna for her son.

Roderick (German)
Famous ruler.

Rodney (English)
Island clearing.

Rodolfo (Spanish)
Bold wolf.

Rodrigo A Spanish
form of Roderick.

Rogelio (Spanish)
Famous warrior.

Roger (German)
Renowned spearman.

Rohan (Irish) Red.

Roland (German)
Famous throughout the
land. *Rolando*

Rollo (Latin) Fame, wolf.
From the name Roul.

Roman (Latin)
One from Rome.

Romeo (Italian) From
Rome. Perhaps the most
romantic name ever on
account of its link with the
Shakespearean character.

Ronald (English)
Powerful advisor. *Ronnie*

Ronan (Irish) Little seal.

Ronin (Hebrew) Song,
joy.

Rory (Irish) Red king.

Ross (Scottish)
Upland, peninsula.

Rowan (Irish) Red.
Rowen

Rowdy A word name
meaning loud, disorderly.

Roy (Irish) Red.

Royal A regal word name
with French roots.

Royce (American)
Roy's son.

Ruairí (ROR-ree) (Irish)
Red-haired king.

Ruaridh (Scottish)
Red-haired king.

Rudolph (German)
Famous wolf. Also a
famous reindeer. *Rudy*

The gift of a name is one of the most precious a parent first bestows upon their child.

ANONYMOUS

Rufus (Latin) Red-haired.

Rugby (English) Rock fortress.

Rumer A unisex name associated with female author Rumer Godden.

Rune (Scandinavian) Secret lore.

Rupert (German) Bright fame. Popular in the UK.

Russell (French) Redhead.

Rusty (French) Red-haired.

Ryan (Irish) Little king. Has been steadily popular since the 1970s.

Ryder (English) Horseman. Derived from the name Rider.

Rylan (English) Land of rye. *Ryland*

Ryker (German) Rich; ruler.

Saber (French) Sword.

Sabino (Latin)
From the Sabines.

Sadler (English)
Saddle maker.

Sage (Latin) Wise, knowing.

Sailor A seafaring
occupational name.

Salvador (Latin) Saviour.
Salvatore, *Sal*

Samir (Arabic)
A pleasant friend.

Samson (Hebrew) Sun. A biblical judge who received superhuman strength.

Samuel (Hebrew) Told by God. A classic biblical name. *Sam*

Santiago (Spanish) Saint. The capital of Chile.

Santos (Spanish)
The saints.

Sargent (French) Officer.

Saul (Hebrew) Desired; prayed for.

Sawyer (English)
Woodworker.

Scott (English) One from Scotland.

Seamus (Irish) Supplanter.

Sean (Irish) God is good. *Shaun, Shawn*

Seanan (Irish) Old and wise.

Sebastian (Latin)
Venerable; respected.

Sedgwick (English)
Sword place.

Selby (English)
From the willow farm.

Selwyn (Latin)
From the woods.

Semaj Created by spelling the name James in reverse.

Sergio (Latin) Servant.

Seth (Hebrew) To appoint.

Seven The number; this name was referenced in the sitcom *Seinfeld*.

Seymour (French)
From St Maur.

Shane (Irish) God is good. Derived from John.

Shaw (English)
Grove of trees.

Shay (Irish) Supplanter. A variation of Seamus.

Shea (English) Stately.

Sheldon (English)
Steep valley.

Sheridan (Irish) Wild one.

Sherlock (English) Bright hair. Used by Conan Doyle for his detective Sherlock Holmes.

Shia (Hebrew)
Praise God.

Sidney (English) Popular in England since the 16th century for its link with the poet Philip Sidney.

Silas (Greek) Wood. *Sylas*

Silver A metallic word name.

Silvester (Latin) Wood, forest.

Simeon (Hebrew)
Harkening.

Simon (Hebrew)
God hears.

Sincere An old-fashioned virtue name still in use today.

Sinclair (French)
From St Clair.

Skip (Scandinavian)
Sea captain.

Skyler (English) Scholar.
Skylar

Slade (English) Valley.

Slater (English)
Slate maker.

Solomon (Hebrew)
Peaceable.

Sonny (English) Son.

Soren (Irish) Apart.

Spencer (English)
Seller of goods.

Spruce A nature name
that also means tidy.

Stafford (English)
From a ford.

Stanley (English)
Stony meadow.

Stefan (Greek) Crowned.
Stefano

Stellan (German) Still,
peaceful.

Sterling (English)
First class.

Steven (Greek) Garland,
crown. *Steve*, *Stephen*

Stone (English) Stalwart.

Storm A powerful force
of nature.

Stuart (Scottish)
Steward. *Stewart*

Sullivan (Irish)
Black-eyed.

Sutton (English) From
the southern homestead.

Sven (Norse) Youth.

Tab A created name made popular by actor Tab Hunter.

Tadhg (TI-ge) (Irish) Poet.

Tafari (African) He who inspires awe.

Taggart (Irish) Son of the priest.

Tahmid (Arabic) Praising.

Tahoma (Native American) Shoreline.

Takeshi (Japanese)
Bamboo.

Talbot (English)
Command of the valley.
A surname.

Talman (Hebrew) Injured.

Talon (French) Claw of
a bird of prey.

Tan (Vietnamese) New.

Tanix (Spanish) Strength.

Tanner (English)
One who tans leather.

Tarquin A Roman clan
name.

Tate (English) Happy.

Taurus (Latin) Bull.
A sign of the Zodiac.

Tavi (Hebrew) Good.

Taylor (English) Tailor.
An occupational name
used for both genders.

Teagan (Irish) Little poet.

Teague (Scottish)
Bard; poet.

Tefo (African) Payment.

Teilo (TAY-lo) (Welsh)
Worthy.

Temple A place of
worship. *Templeton*

Tennessee A Native
American place name.

Terrance A Latin tribal
name. *Terence*

Terrell (German)
Follower of Thor.

Teva (Hebrew) Nature.

Thackeray An English
surname associated
with author William
Makepeace Thackeray.

Thaddeus (Aramaic)
Brave. *Tad*

Thayer (French) Tailor.

Theodore (Greek) Gift
of God. *Ted*, *Teddy*, *Theo*

Thomas (Aramaic) Twin.
A classic biblical name.
Tomas, *Tommy*, *Tom*

Thor (Scandinavian)
Thunder. Very popular
in Denmark.

Thurston (Scandinavian)
Thor's stone.

Tiago (Spanish)
St James. Short form
of Santiago.

Tibet An Asian place
name.

Tiernan (Irish) Little lord.

Tiger The animal;
brought to fame by golfer
Tiger Woods.

Tilden (English)
Fertile valley.

Timothy (Greek)
Honouring God. A classic
name from the New
Testament. *Timmy*

Timur (Hebrew) Tall.

Titus (Greek) To honour.

Tobias (Hebrew)
God is good. *Toby*

Todd (English) Fox.

*Love is flower-like;
Friendship is like a
sheltering tree.*

SAMUEL TAYLOR
COLERIDGE

Tony (Latin) Praiseworthy.
Short form of Anthony.

Topaz A gemstone.

Trace A modern name
meaning 'small amount'
or 'to follow'.

Travis (French) Toll taker.

Tremaine (Celtic)
Stone house.

Trent (Latin)
Rushing waters.

Trenton (Latin)
Trent's town.

Trevon A creative twist
on the name Trevor.

Trevor (Welsh) From
the large homestead.

Trey (English) Three.

Tripp (English) Third son.

Tristan (Celtic) Tumult;
riot. *Tristen, Tristian,
Tristin, Triston*

Troy (Irish) Soldier.
The legendary setting
of the Trojan war.

Tucker (English)
Fabric worker.

Turner (English)
Woodworker.

Twain (English) Divided
in two. Associated with
author and humourist
Mark Twain.

Ty A pet form of names
beginning with Ty.

Tyler (English) Tile maker.

Tynan (Irish) Dark.

Tyree (Scottish)
From Tyrie.

Tyrell (Latin) Roman
tribal name.

Tyrone (Irish)
Land of Owen.

Tyson (English)
Firebrand.

The stylish Irish

You may look no further than the Emerald Isle for the inspiration behind many of today's most popular boys' names. The choices are perfect for those looking for a modern-sounding name with a rich heritage. Some of them are already quite popular, while others are gems waiting to be discovered.

Aiden	Cullen	Kellen
Breccan	Declan	Logan
Brennan	Dillon	Mannix
Brian	Donovan	Nolan
Caden	Eamon	Patrick
Cale	Finn	Quinlan
Casey	Garrett	Rowan
Cian	Gilby	Ryan
Kian	Grady	Sean
Connor	Keegan	Sullivan

Scottish stand-outs

Scotland is a country famous for its castle-dotted highlands, historic battle sites, and its whisky. But if you love the sound of Scottish Gaelic names, you are also in good company. They are masculine, a bit mischievous, and fitting for both your active little boy and the man he'll grow up to become.

Aberdeen	Guthrie
Angus	Ian
Brody	Kyle
Bruce	Lachlan
Callen	Macaulay
Cameron	Maxwell
Colin	Teague
Craig	Tyree
Dashiell	Wallace
Duncan	Wylie
Grant	

boys

UV

Udell An English surname meaning yew-tree grove.

Ulan (African) Firstborn twins.

Uleki The Hawaiian form of Ulysses.

Ulric (German) Wolf power.

Ultan (Irish) Man from Ulster.

Ulysses (Latin) Wrathful. A character in ancient Greek literature. *Ulises*

Umberto (Italian) Famous German.

Unique An unsubtle word name.

Urban (Latin) Man from the city.

Uriah (Hebrew) God is my light. *Urijah*

Uriel (Hebrew) God is my light.

Usher (English) Doorkeeper.

Utah A place name referring to the western U.S. state.

Uziah (Hebrew) God is my strength.

Vachel (French) Small cow.

Valentin (Latin) Strong. *Valentino*

Valerio (Latin) Healthy.

Valour A word name meaning great bravery.

Van (Dutch) Shortened version of Evan and Ivan.

Vance (English) One who lives near the marsh.

Vasant (Hindu) Spring.

Vaughan (Welsh) Small. *Vaughn*

Venedict (Russian) Blessed.

Verlin (American) Spring.

Vernon (French) Alder tree.

Vicente The Spanish form of Vincent.

Victor (Latin) Conqueror.

Viggo (Scandinavian) War.

Vihaan (Sanskrit) First ray of light.

Vincent (Latin) Conqueror. *Vincenzo*

Virgil (Latin) Staff bearer.

Vito (Latin) Alive.

Von (Scandinavian) Hope.

Voss (Old Norse) Wave; sea.

WX

Wade (English)
At a river crossing.

Wakeley (English)
Damp meadow.

Walden (German)
To rule.

Walker (English)
Cloth-worker; walker.
Associated with the
American TV drama
Walker, Texas Ranger.

Wallace (Scottish) One from Wales; also linked with Scottish patriot William Wallace.

Walter (German) Ruler of the people. *Walt*

Ward (English) Guard; watchman.

Warner (English) Army.

Warren (German) Protector.

Warrick (English) Fortress.

Warwick (English) House near a dam.

Watson (English) Son of Walter.

Waylon (English) Meadow of aspen trees.

Wayne (English) Wagon maker.

Webster (English) Weaver.

Wendell (German) Wanderer; traveller. *Wendall*, *Wendal*, *Wendel*,

Wesley (English) Western meadow. *Wes*

West A newly fashionable word name.

Weston (English) Western town. *Westin*

Wheeler (English) A wheel maker.

Whitby (English) A farm with white walls.

Wilbur (German) Brilliant.

Wiley (English) Water meadow.

William (German) Constant protector. A longstanding classic. *Bill*, *Vilhelm*, *Willem*, *Will*, *Willis*, *Willie*

Willoughby (English) Willow-tree farm.

Wilson (English) Son of Will.

Winston (English) Friend's town.

Wit (Polish) Life.

Wolfgang (German) Travelling wolf. Mozart's first name. *Wolf*

Woodrow (English) A lane in the woods. *Woody*

Wray (Scandinavian) Dweller from the corner.

Wyatt (English) Strength in war. Borne by famed gunman Wyatt Earp.

Wylie A Scottish form of William.

Wystan (English) Battle stone.

X

Xadrian A created form of Adrian.

Xander A diminutive of Alexander.

Xavi (Basque) New house.

Xavier (Basque) New house. *Xzavier*

Xenos (Greek) Guest.

Yadiel (Latin)
Beloved friend.

Yahir (Spanish) Handsome.
Popularized by the Mexican
singer Yahir Othón Parra.

Yale (English) Up on the
hill. Surname and Ivy
League university.

Yandel (Spanish)
A variation of Llandel.

Yarden (Hebrew)
To flow down, descend.

Yardley (English)
Enclosed meadow.

Yates An English surname
meaning gates.

Yehuda (Hebrew) Praise.
Yehudi

Yonah A Hebrew variation
of Jonah.

York (English) Yew tree.

Yosef (Hebrew)
God will increase. *Yusuf*

Yule (English) Christmas.

Yves (French) Yew wood.

Z

Zacchaeus (Hebrew)
Pure.

Zachariah (Hebrew) The
Lord has remembered.

Zachary (Hebrew) The
Lord has remembered.
Zackery, Zach, Zac

Zaide (Hebrew) Older.

Zaiden A modern
variation of Zaide.

Zaire An African place
name.

Zander (Greek)
Protector. A variant
spelling of Xander.

Zane (English) God is
gracious; linked with
author Zane Grey. *Zain*

Zared (Hebrew)
He descends.

Zavier (Basque)
New house.

Zayden A new take on
the name Aiden.

Zeal A word name
meaning energy.
enthusiasm.

Zealand (Scandinavian)
From the sea land.

Zebediah (Hebrew)
Gift of Jehovah.

Zebulon (Hebrew)
To give honour.

Zeke (Hebrew)
Strength of God.

Zen Word name referring
to the Japanese school
of Buddhism.

Zenith (English) The
highest celestial point
above an observer.

Zephyr (Greek) West
wind; gentle breeze.

Zion (Hebrew)
Promised land.

Zyler A modern variation
of Tyler.

boys

Photography credits

Vanessa Davies
page 36

Christopher Drake
pages 17, 32, 72, 81

Winfried Heinze
pages 16, 24

Emma Mitchell
pages 50, 106

Daniel Pangbourne
page 40

Claire Richardson
pages 10, 28, 76, 109, 116

Polly Wreford
pages 1, 4, 5, 6, 8–9, 20, 31, 34, 38, 43,
46, 61, 64, 68, 74, 78, 89, 90, 94, 98,
100, 105, 110, 120, 122, 124, 126, 127,
130, 131, 134, 140, 144

Debi Treloar
pages 3, 26, 55, 57, 58, 103, 114, 119,
133, 136, 138, 142

page 2 ©Stockbyte

Acknowledgments

Thanks to my family and in particular my
parents, who gave me a wonderful name.
Also to my friends who share my affection for
names: Heather, Rebecca, Emily and Brandy.
Where would I be without Ryan's sounding
board? And his dinners? Thank you.